LIVE TO TELL

LIVE TO TELL

A NIGHTMARE ON GAY STREET

A Memoir

DAVID TALAMANTES

iUniverse, Inc.
New York Bloomington Shanghai

LIVE TO TELL
A NIGHTMARE ON GAY STREET

iUniverse books may be ordered through booksellers or by contacting:

iUniverse
1663 Liberty Drive
Bloomington, IN 47403
www.iuniverse.com
1-800-Authors (1-800-288-4677)

ISBN: 978-0-595-42976-9 (pbk)
ISBN: 978-0-595-87317-3 (ebk)

Printed in the United States of America

Preface

I never imagined myself writing a book, especially one about the events of my life. I've never thought that what I've lived through is anything interesting enough for someone else to want to read about it. But that was before I lived through these recent years. It's been one hell of a journey. When the hell was finally over, when I could finally see no direct evidence that the dark forces were still surrounding me, I realized that maybe it was over. And it was then that I began to heal my heart, mind, and body. It was then that I knew I had saved myself.

My nightmare began in the fall of 2002. Nearly two years later, I managed to pull out of my downward spiral at the very last minute, regain control, and somehow land safely. Since then, through my healing, mind-clearing, and personal discovery, I've come to understand the invisible forces that took over my world. I now know what stole into my life. And I journeyed to this end loud enough to ensure that I lived to talk about it, or at least that's how I explain the craziness to myself. I was a lost soul back then. I have no idea how I managed to survive. I know I'm not the only one to fall into their heinous web, and I pray I'm not the only one to escape it. With the telling of my story, I hope others realize what they are caught up in, I hope their loved ones realize what is happening, and I hope I provide clues and a voice for those desperate souls so they may save themselves. I also hope I encourage a community of survivors to band together and put an end to this unspoken evil.

I want to emphasize the fact that what I have written in this book is true, not exaggeration, literary license, or any other form of stretching of the truth. Through my journey, at the mercy of helpless distortions by this network of thieves, I've grown to understand the importance of truth, even simple truth. White lies are no more acceptable than any other lie. I now know that it is important to live life honestly, something I don't think many people really understand or honor. In this book, I shine a light upon my own life, to clear my darkness and to reveal the darkness that has touched my life.

"It is better to die on your feet
Than to live on your knees."

—*José Martí*

The Box is Opened

I guess the place to start is at the beginning, the beginning of what has been one hell of a ride. A journey I struggle to understand, but one I now embrace and own, for this is my story.

Hell for me began a few years ago, the summer of 2002, not long after moving out of the Seattle suburbs and back into the city with my partner Jeff. This move was our eleventh-hour attempt to hold onto the love and relationship we had shared for over a decade. Somehow during the latter part of those years, we lost the spark that had fueled the flame of a wondrously happy and exciting marriage of souls.

For me, it was hard to know exactly what went wrong; maybe it was the 13 years' age difference or the changing, fading sexual energy we both were experiencing. Maybe it was all the years of living out in lonely suburbia. My lifelong struggle with low self-esteem and social anxiety might have been the string that was unraveling it all. After all, it was I who struggled to find a reason not to give up and leave. It was I who was so desperately troubled by the problems we were having. I guess it was all of those things and more. We were both searching for that magical potion that would take away the sense that something was missing for us.

Though we'd only been back in the city for a short time, the excitement had already begun to fade, just as anything new in life does. The colors begin to dull, the music slowly fades, and the euphoria comes to an end. I was left with the same hollow feeling that I had run to the city to escape. At first I was sure I had shaken it, but once again it had found me, just as it had in every other place I'd run to. Why could I never break free from it and hold onto my desire for lasting happiness? Happiness was like a shadow for me, teasing me with its presence but disappearing whenever I shone my light upon it.

"Let's go out tonight," I say from my slouched position on the sofa, staring out into the night. As I sit there, my eyes are focused on the fantastic view of the Space Needle beyond the windows of our apartment. I wonder how many happy gay boys with friends at parties are staring out at the same incredible view, with their music wafting through the air, ice cubes clinking as they toast their blessedness, their laughter billowing out the windows. It's a view that once promised Jeff and me all of these things. On this night, it just reminds me of how lonely I still am.

"We live seven blocks from the clubs and we never go out," I say.

"We go out. Why do you think we never go out?" Jeff asks. He sits there in his recliner still glowing in the happiness he thinks this move has provided us. He holds desperately on to that happiness because if he were to let go of it, he'd lose what he loves most about his life: me.

I know that, and I don't want to cause him that pain, but my anger is growing louder than his fear. My sense that life is passing me by is beginning to scream so much louder than his breaking heart does. I know something is going to snap under this pressure, I just don't know when it will happen or what it will look like. I know it's coming and I am afraid.

"I don't know," I say, "it just feels like we don't. I'm tired of sitting here in this apartment, staring at the walls and listening to everyone around us having fun all the time. We moved here to have fun again, Jeff, not to sit at home. This is what we did when we lived in Bonney Lake. Sitting in this apartment isn't fun for me. Is it fun for you?"

"All right, I hear what you're saying. And you're right. We should get out more. Come on, let's go play." He jumps up, all 6 feet, 200 lbs of his quarterback self, kicks the footrest away, bends over and grabs my hand, eager to make me happy, desperate to provide the answers I long for. I resist, still staring out into the night. Get mad at me, damn it! Fight me! Aren't you tired of my anger? Why won't you give up like I'm giving up? I can't do this alone, I need your help.

Even though I got what I asked for that night, part of me continued to feel sad and angry. That unhappiness ran deeper than Jeff was aware of and I knew it couldn't be solved with that one victory. Privately, I was developing a new despair about my life that I hadn't yet shared with him. Witnessing the apparent happiness and freedom that so many single gay boys in the city seemed to be enjoying had become more tormenting than the isolation that suburbia had ever been for me. I still loved Jeff deeply, but I also longed for what appeared all around me—a happiness that seemed exclusive to the independent.

As the world inside me was changing, the world around me had begun to change too. With the advent of the Internet, the planet was shrinking, evolving. Everything was suddenly right there at your fingertips. What's important to my story is the ability to connect with and communicate with any person anywhere. And with that, you could now order up sex and pseudo-love, like take-out from the local Thai restaurant. No longer did you have to venture out into the cold and shuffle through endless bodies until the right pheromone spark occurred. With the Internet, you could hone in on exactly what and whom you were looking for, not unlike the way a heat-seeking missile locates and connects with its intended target. No more getting dressed up and walking around smoky, noisy bars in search of a person with whom you might luckily have one thing in common, much less actually make a love connection with. No, those days were long gone. Now you could sit at your computer wearing anything you wanted, doing anything you wanted, while visiting the countless websites, searching through the profiles of the thousands of others who were there for the same purpose of lust and love. Or God knows what else.

When we get to the end-stage of a failed marriage, we are often willing to try things and go places that previously seemed impossible. Feelings of worthlessness and hopelessness can sometimes open doors we wish had never been discovered, much less stepped through. These doors presented themselves to me, and after years of struggling through every attempt and failure I could, I desperately reached out and opened them, one by one by one.

The opening of one of these doors presented a new constitution for Jeff and me, and one that we quickly embraced. We decided to try an open relationship. Our friendship was fine, so maybe an innocent booty call once in a while was all we needed to live happily together. Sex had always been very pleasurable and important in my life, and the lack of it had left an emptiness that was hard to bear. I didn't understand, I didn't want to understand, why I was no longer sexually desired by Jeff. I'd heard about couples losing the desire to have sex with each other after years of marriage, but that was not us. It couldn't be. We were both attractive men with healthy sex drives.

At the same time, it seemed that everyone around us had thrown monogamy and caution to the wind, choosing instead to feast on the endless supply of lonely, horny souls available with just the click of a mouse. Witnessing this, we decided that it was okay for us to do the same.

"I think we should give this chat thing a chance," I say. It's late and I should be working, but this newly discovered cyber-world has just deposited its irresistible hook into my life. My projects and lists of deadlines are strewn about my desk, the flashing light on my answering machine is begging for my attention, the Space Needle glows beautifully outside my office window, but my distraction is complete.

"There are so many guys on here, even couples like us. And the guys are hot! Look at this, Jeff."

He leans in and watches as I click through the profiles and photos of several of the hundreds of gay men who are currently logged into the website. There are single men, couples, some wanting boyfriends, but most just wanting to get laid—and quickly. And so many of them are young, beautiful guys, not anyone I would imagine having to advertise for sex.

"This list here, this is everyone who wants to hook up for sex *right now*. And look at this. They even have nude pictures."

"Wow, all of those guys are online right now looking for sex?" Jeff asks.

It doesn't take long for him to get excited by what he sees. It wouldn't take long for any gay man with eyeballs and a decent amount of testosterone flowing through his system to get excited by this.

"Yup, all of them, like ordering pizza," I say.

Jeff then proceeds with the interrogation.

"How did you find out about this?"

"I saw an ad in the *Seattle Gay News*. I decided to check it out, and here we are."

"How long has this been going on?" he asks.

"I don't know. From the looks of it, I'd guess a while. Look at the graphics. This is a sophisticated website. And with all these people, it can't be new. This took some serious money, time, and planning."

"Have *you* hooked up with anyone on here?" he asks.

I see the worry in his eyes.

"No," I reply. "I just created my profile last night."

"It's okay if you have," he says.

"Jeff, we talked about this. It's not going to work if we're not completely honest about everything."

"Have you chatted with anyone?" He now seems to be losing the eagerness we'd just been sharing about all this.

I hesitate, and then continue. "Yea, a couple people last night after I logged in. You have to create a profile to get in. But I don't have any pictures posted, so nobody seems all that interested in me." I close the remaining windows and quit my browser, realizing the night of fun has come to an end.

"Are you going to post your picture?" he asks.

"I'm thinking about it. Are you sure you're okay with this?" I turn off the monitor and spin my chair to face him.

"Yes. Don't worry. Nothing has changed. We both agreed that this is what we want."

"I know, but it just feels weird now that it's happening. When we talked about having an open relationship, we didn't know about this website. Either of us could have sex with someone right now if we wanted to. I didn't realize it would happen so fast." I lean forward, look down, and place my hands upon his knees, suddenly worried myself about where we're heading.

"Well, do you still want to do this?" he asks.

"Yea, I guess. I just don't want to hurt you. And I don't want to hurt us." I look back into his eyes, looking for something to comfort me.

"Dave, stop worrying. It really is okay. I know how much you love me and I know you would never hurt me. This is just sex. Let's enjoy it. Have fun." He wraps his arms around me and gives me a long hard hug. Hugging has always been our way of checking in with each other, our way of verifying that everything really is okay.

With that discussion, we take the first steps, and quickly the insatiable appetite for this endless menu begins to numb the pain that had driven us to this new world. In no time, I find myself spending every free minute staring into this window of flesh, picking and choosing with whom I might enjoy this new experience. *Social anxiety and insecurity, go back to your room! You aren't needed here.*

I can now be whomever I want. Even when I invite someone over or get invited to play with someone else, it's not like any real conversation is going to happen anyhow. That doesn't seem to be the goal on this playground. Who would have ever imagined that the Internet would provide this?

Though I only experienced a handful of actual hookups, I talked my way through many that could have been. In the online chat sex hookup world, virtual expectation trumps reality. Based on my experience, and I think mine was a good barometer of what was going on, I'd guess the percentage of physical contact was relatively low when you added up the hours spent fishing for it. I think the fishing becomes a big part of the hook and pleasure though. It's definitely addicting. You realize that within the first minutes when you log on and see the list of the hundreds in your city who are there too.

If it weren't exciting on some level, there wouldn't be so many people doing it. Could it be another version of gambling? "I'm one hit away from the big one." Twenty-first century foreplay. It's an element of the evolution of sex, or so I've been told.

"What are you doing right now?" Jordan asks.

"Not much, just hanging at home today. You?"

"Just wrapping up the details of a couple cases I'm working on."

"Cases? Are you an attorney?"

"Yep. I'm a city prosecutor. Are you home alone?"

"Yea. I am."

He is a very beautiful man. I think about everything that I've just learned about this stranger. It seems surprising but exciting that I am about to have an anonymous hookup and with someone who isn't trashy. This was my first hookup, and privately, I was still struggling with the feeling that this was wrong. Finding out that he was a professional like me was all I needed to feel better about it and about myself. And so began my plunge into the deep end of the pool.

After a few months of playing in the water, reality hit. Just like all things in my past, this too began to fizzle out, sputtering like a parched gas-guzzler in the middle of a trek through the desert. And this could mean only one thing. The enemy was back; my monster had found me again. Fear, depression, insecurity and everything else low self-esteem had always forced upon me had returned. And with this, I began to realize that empty, nameless sex wasn't going to defeat it. My troubles would require something much more powerful.

So I started looking for love, even though I didn't really understand that that was what I was pursuing. I knew I needed to fill that empty hollow place inside me with something more than just sex. Jeff and I weren't having sex anymore, so we looked outside ourselves to fulfill that missing piece. But it wasn't so easy for me. My mind told me that I needed all of it, the whole package, and I needed all of it to come from one source. So I changed my strategy and began searching for something deeper, something more meaningful and, at the same time, more desperate. Rather than the empty calories of drive-thru carnal eating, I began to look for a hookup with substance, someone with traits other than just a hot body and big hands. I was looking for a boyfriend. That special someone who'd make love to me *and* make me feel good about myself again. I wanted someone to cherish my mind and my body. I needed someone who could scare away the dark entity chasing after me. And thanks to the Internet, it happened almost overnight.

Love at First Sight

I take one last look in the mirror, and then grab my keys and head out the door. I hold my arms away from my body as I make my way down the hall to the elevator, hoping the passing air will dry my pits. The anxiety is overwhelming now. My heart is pounding, my mind is racing, and I just want to turn around and forget going through with it.

"There is nothing to be afraid of, David. He's going to like you." I say to myself, not believing a single word of it. I can imagine him seeing my nervousness and thinking I'm strange because of it.

Seth and I had been chatting online for over a month, but it had taken this long for me to develop the courage to meet in person. It's easier getting to know someone as you hide behind the veil of your computer connection. For me, it took much more nerve to feel comfortable enough to take this huge step of meeting in person, without the goal of silent sex. Sexual encounters are easy compared to this. Getting to know someone, revealing your true self, takes so much more courage.

I get into my new black Nissan 350Z, turn the key, and hear the deep throaty roar of the engine. This brings a smile to my face. Surely he'll be impressed when he sees me in this. It takes a successful person to afford a car like this. Everyone likes successful people.

The restaurant is just a few blocks from my apartment, but I decide to drive because being in my car gives me a sense of security. And I can use the air conditioning to dry my armpits. No doubt he'll lose interest if I show up with sweaty armpits. As I drive the short distance to the Deluxe Bar & Grill, I continue to coach myself, though it doesn't seem to help much. *God, why me? Of all the burdens I could have, why do I have to be the one to suffer with this damn anxiety? Why can't I be normal like everyone else?*

It's in the beginning of any socializing, during the explosion of anxiety, that my monster arrives, splashing in with the chemicals that begin to pour from my hypothalamus. He and his friends, Fear and Worthlessness, come to party like its New Year's, drinking up like an alcoholic on a binge. Once they arrive, I'm in defense mode, doing everything I can not to crumble and run away in defeat. It's during all of this that I have to find calm, composure, charm, intelligence, humor, and everything else I need to appear like a normal social butterfly. At that oh-so-important moment of first impression, a chemical weapon attack has just gone off in my body, and I can't say one word about it or give any signal that anything is wrong. Welcome to my life.

I drive around the block several times looking for a curbside spot. There are several pay lots near the restaurant, but this is really just a delay tactic to put off the inevitable meeting I'm about to suffer through. Realizing I'm already late, I give in and park in a lot. As I run across the sweltering street and into the restaurant, my head begins to spin as I realize I'm actually going through with it. Show-time!

After searching the restaurant in an adrenaline-induced haze, I recognize Seth sitting at a booth toward the back. The Deluxe is popular with the locals of Capital Hill, a neighborhood that Seattle's gay community calls home. Wrapped in dark wood paneling and lush lighting, with a large ornate bar at its heart, the Deluxe plays host to a dependably young, lively atmosphere most anytime of the day or night.

"Hi, Seth?"

"Yea, are you David?"

I nod and thrust my hand out for a polite shake. He takes my hand and casually looks around the room as if to see who might be watching. He seems concerned by the attention of those around us. This seems odd to me. I quickly take a seat and grab one of the menus on the table. The waiter comes and I order a Tanqueray Gin Martini. He orders a Cosmopolitan. Though I know we don't plan to order food, I pretend to examine the menu to keep myself distracted from the awkwardness of the moment.

Our drinks arrive, and I take a big gulp. We then start to talk. With the warmth of the alcohol beginning to soothe my nerves, I am able to look at him with lessening fear. Alcohol has often been the substance that eases my anxiety. I'd never had the courage to work with a therapist about my fears. I guess I feared the perceived weakness more than the ailment.

I take a deep breath and assess my surroundings, hoping to find something to calm my nerves. I take another drink. I can now look directly at him, and this time I don't look away. He's taller than I imagined he'd be, nearly six feet, but thin. He doesn't look like the pictures he showed me, but I find him attractive anyway. His hair is blond like the pictures, his lips are plump like the pictures, and he has deep blue eyes like the pictures. But he doesn't look like the pictures. Wondering if the same is true for me, I suddenly worry that I'm not his type. I have a nice body and a hot little platinum blond Caesar cut, just like the pictures. I've been working out very intensely for over six months. I look good, though I've never had the confidence to truly believe such a thing about myself, especially when being scrutinized by another. My social phobias have been quite effective in preventing me from developing much of an ego.

Little did I know that I was staring at a man who would soon begin to fulfill every wish I could think of, even before I could verbalize them, as if he somehow knew my very thoughts. As we sat in that restaurant, breaking down the wall of Strangers, the life I had always known was beginning to churn, a light breeze just rustling the dust of 34 years. And I had not one clue of the hell that was coming my way.

After a couple of drinks, light conversation, and what feels like sincere smiles from Seth, I decide things are going well, and wanting my lucky streak to continue, I offer him a ride back to his apartment. Good time to introduce the car. He likes it. As we drive to his place, I wonder if he'll invite me in. If he does, I'm a stud. If not, I'm such a loser. He invites me in. Yes, there is a God!

"Welcome to my little home," he says.

It's a very small studio apartment, a bathroom off to the left and a galley kitchen directly ahead. A few feet beyond the bath and to the left is the living room, a narrow expanse with a small black-and-white stripped couch, a pine entertainment cabinet, and a queen-size bed in the back corner. Other than the couch, the furniture is kind of rustic, vaguely Southwestern, and somewhat dated. Everything has a very 80s feel to it. Just past the kitchen, where a dining room would normally be, is a desk and computer. I notice a bottle of lubricant next to the monitor. I smile, realizing this is where he'd been sitting during all of our chats. Beyond that, sliding doors lead to the courtyard. There are dishes piled in the sink and clothes strewn about. I get the sense he doesn't like doing chores very much. Feeling uncomfortable, I quickly attempt to hide what I'm noticing about his life.

"So, you're not going to believe this, but I live in the next building over."

"Are you serious? The Bellecourt?"

"Yea, how weird is that?"

"That is weird. Then why did you drive to the restaurant if you live so close?"

"I don't know. I like to drive, I guess."

"That's silly. Here, have a seat on the couch." He grabs the pile of clean laundry and throws it on the bed. "Would you like something to drink? I don't have any alcohol though. I'm not much of a drinker."

"Water's fine." He heads to the kitchen. As I sit, I notice movement on the bed. "You have a cat!"

"Yea, his name is Diva," he yells from the kitchen.

"What a great name. Is he gay?"

"That's funny."

"I'm allergic to cats," I quickly add.

"Oh, I'm sorry. Do you need to leave?"

"Maybe not. We'll know soon enough if I start sneezing uncontrollably. I probably shouldn't pet him though."

He laughs, then returns from the kitchen, hands me a glass of water, and sits down next to me. Diva jumps into his lap and he plays with him. I pray I don't start sneezing. After a few minutes, he tosses him to the floor and turns back to me. I feel awkward and speechless. To my relief, he keeps the conversation moving with an endless flow of irrelevant small talk about himself. As I'm listening to his words, watching his lips move, my heart starts pounding and my stomach tightens. I'm overcome with the desire to kiss him.

"Would I be out of line if I asked you for a kiss?" I interrupt.

He appears surprised and oddly looks up and around the room, as though communicating to an unknown audience. He then looks back at me, smiles, and says "No."

I look around trying to understand what he has just done, and then I look back into his eyes and boldly lean in, cup his face in my hands, and put my lips to his. My heart is exploding and I can't believe my sudden courage. After a few minutes of deep kissing, I suddenly become embarrassed and pull away. He looks around again, smiling, and then looks back at me.

"Well, I'd better get going," I say.

"Yea, it's getting late."

We stand. I lean in and give him a quick hug, then quickly escape out the door. The night is a success and I'm on top of the world. Ha! I win this battle.

During the next week, Seth and I talked on the phone each evening, getting to know each other a little more with each conversation. Because of my shyness, the talks were quite short, but he was gentle and very friendly, and that made me feel more at ease than I would have with most people at such an early phase. I wasn't spending nearly as much time on the Internet now. This gave me some much-needed time to catch up on my freelance work projects and more time with Jeff. Since discovering the website, we hadn't made much time for each other, so it was nice to have some dinners and conversation together.

The following weekend, Seth invited me to join him and his friends out at Neighbours, a gay dance bar popular with the locals and the younger circuit-party scene. Circuit boys are a network of mostly gay partiers who gather at clubs and lavish dance events known for their elaborate music, lighting, and theme décor. Drugs are also a big part of the culture. Although I was nervous about going there alone, I was also excited at the prospect of having a boyfriend, a social life, and some sense of genuine happiness again. Somehow, I was sure these things would nail the coffin shut on my monster once and for all.

That weekend would also be my first taste of partying like a Rock Star. From the many hours of chatting we'd done online over the month before we met in person, I was aware that Seth participated in the circuit scene, including the various club drugs, but from what he'd said about it, I assumed it wasn't anything extreme. I remember being a little concerned about this, but not so much that it affected the way I felt about him. Having experimented a little myself throughout my life, none of what he described to me seemed frightening. I believed that club drugs weren't used in the way heroin addicts, speed freaks, cokeheads, or junkies used drugs. In the gay club scene, it was very much about looking fabulous, feeling even more fabulous, dancing and mingling and partying the night away. Then heading home, and going to bed. End of story. Boy, was I ever wrong! For an outsider, it might look wonderful watching all the hot boys at the club, smiling and dancing, covered in glitter and wearing sexy little outfits on their buff gorgeous bodies, booty shaking till dawn. But if you watched really close, you might catch the occasional tragic queen who was losing control and making a complete mess of himself, as they all eventually do. Usually though, his ever-present group of accomplices would cart him away before most people noticed the train wreck. It seemed to be an unwritten rule in the scene, mostly because one messy boy could ruin it for everyone. If it happened too often, the bar acted quickly to start 86-ing those who couldn't behave.

As I pull into the parking lot of the club that night, I'm feeling the full effect of an anxiety attack that has grown stronger as I've moved closer to this moment of eager dread. Feeling wounded and vulnerable, I quietly slide the car into a stall and turn off my engine. I sit in silence for a while, attempting to talk myself down. I can hear the deep bass pumping out through the walls of the old brick building, begging me to come play. I see boys coming and going, laughing as they sashay back and forth. *God, I hate this fear.* Finally, I take one last look in the rear view mirror, run my fingers through the front of my hair, smile at myself through sad, desperate eyes, and then groan in agony as I open the door and step out. As I hear the door slam behind me, a sudden rush of adrenaline pounds through my already overwhelmed head. *Oh God, please help me get through this!*

I walk up to the entrance and take my place in line. I manage a smile as I look about the crowd gathered outside, pretending as best I can not to be afraid. A few boys look me up and down and then smile back at me, attempting to gain my attention. This feels good, though I only have enough courage to return a quick smile before I look away. *Good going. Now he probably thinks you're an asshole.* I quickly flash my ID to the doorman, pay the cover charge, and disappear into the darkness beyond.

Once inside, I peruse the club for a while, attempting to get as comfortable as I have any hope of getting before locating Seth. The club is a large cavernous expanse. It's dark; the walls are painted black. The crowded dance floor is in the middle of the two-story warehouse. It is a sea of heads rising and falling to the beat of the music. Above is a canopy of laser lights, high-tech gadgets, and large mirrored disco balls slowly spinning, reflecting focused beams of light into every possible corner of the darkness, splashing for a split second onto each person's face, illuminating their state of being only briefly as it moves through the club. Lining the perimeter, midway up the outer wall is a mezzanine level overlooking everything, an observation deck from which to perch and witness all the sin and skin. The club is crowded, people are milling about everywhere, mostly men in their early 20s and 30s, but a fair number of older guys and some women are there too. The music is incredible. Madonna's *Die Another Day* is roaring in my ears, and the bass begins to pound in my chest. Oh, I love this song!

I suddenly feel very excited and grin in pure pleasure. This is my Disneyland, the incredible gay otherworld that exists just for me, whenever I manage to find it. I have minimal fear in this world. I am not an alien in this world.

I begin to bob my head to the beat and wiggle my hips ever so slightly. I'd love to run out onto the dance floor and let loose with my moves, but that's not happening until I get some alcohol into me to shake me from the spell of my insecurities. I notice a bartender without a line in front of him and as gracefully as possible, I rush to him.

"Hello, sweetie, what can I do for you?" he says through a huge gorgeous smile. I sense his question is a double entendre and feel flustered. I bashfully hesitate. He continues to stare at me, smiling that big smile of his.

"Hi." I return a nervous smile. "Could I get a vodka cranberry, please?"

"Will that be a single or a double, honey?"

"Oh, definitely a double!" I quickly reply.

He laughs and proceeds to mix my drink. "How's your evening so far?" he asks.

"Okay I guess. It'll be better after I have that drink." I say this literally, but he laughs thinking I'm making a clever joke. I smile back but look away when I feel his eyes holding mine too long. He slides my drink across to me; I push him a $10 bill, say thanks, and quickly turn away. I lean forward to keep my drink from splashing down my front as I raise it to my mouth, still trying to bounce to the beat. I pull the straw into my lips and start sucking. After downing nearly half the cocktail, I lower the glass and look around for somewhere to do my best imitation of wallpaper. I see an open spot near the dance floor, so I move into place in front of the railing that separates the floor from the crowd of onlookers. Excited, I watch the sea of floating, shirtless hot bodies drifting around to the beat.

A few minutes later I notice Seth at the far end of the dance floor and my stomach instantly does a double back flip. This is an unmistakable sign that my monster is becoming disturbed. I gulp down the rest of my drink, set the glass on the railing, and then stare back at Seth.

There he is, bouncing around on the dance floor, with those beautiful lights splashing all around him. Wow, he looks really cute! And he's waiting for me to arrive. He's waiting for me!

He's wearing a typical circuit boy uniform: cargo shorts, tank top, visor, "sketchy" sunglasses, a mini neon light stick flipping around in his mouth, and an expression of complete pleasure. He looks flawless.

After watching him dance for a few more minutes, I make the decision to go to him. I feel stronger now, confident. I turn away from the dance floor, work my way through the crowd, and make my way to the opposite end of the club. When I get close to where he is dancing, I stop and stand, watching him move. When he finally notices me, he jumps up and down with excitement, flashes a beautiful smile, and waves me over. I smile and confidently walk to him. I'm so happy right now. He gives me a big hug, grabs my hand, and pulls me with him.

As we approach his group of friends though, I see immediately that they aren't smiling as they watch us. It's as though they feel a shared sense of threat. And with that, my monster arrives. *It's okay. Stay calm*, I silently tell myself.

"David, this is Ray. Ray, David."

I reach out for the polite handshake that doesn't materialize. Ray flashes a smile that is obviously disingenuous, glares at Seth through his phony pleasure, then turns and walks away.

"Bitch," Seth says, watching him go. He then introduces me to Ricky, Peter, Heyden, and Richard. They seem happier to meet me, shaking my hand and giving me hugs. I reciprocate, but I'm still troubled by Ray's actions. I look around trying to find him. I wonder what that was all about. He doesn't know me. But then Seth puts his arm around me and smiles into my eyes. I'm happy again.

"Let's go outside and cool off," Seth yells over the music to the group, pointing to the entrance. Most of the group nods in agreement, though Heyden says he needs to take care of some business and excuses himself. Richard just smiles and walks in the direction Ray took. Seth then takes my hand and leads me through the crowd. Along the way to the exit, he smiles at, hugs, and carries on short conversations with many in our path. He seems to know a lot of people at the club. I'm excited now but intimidated too. I hope he'll still like me when he finds out I'm not so popular.

Once outside, the remainder of the group assembles. Seth ushers me aside, out of the prying eyes of the doorman and the crowd gathered outside. He pulls my hand out and places a small pink pill into my palm.

"I wasn't sure if you wanted this tonight, but I got you one in case you do."

"What is it?" I ask, studying the small object in my hand.

"It's Ecstasy, silly. And it's some really good shit. I'm rolling my ass off right now!"

"Really?" I look up at him and suddenly see the high in his face. I look around and suddenly notice everyone else with that same look in their eyes. Ah, *now* I understand that look he had on the dance floor. I look back at him, then back at the others, then down at the pill. I take a deep breath, look back into his eyes, and smile a nervous smile.

Now I knew where all that pleasure of his was really coming from. It was more than just the music, the club, and the anticipation of me bringing this pleasure to his evening. His joy was being fueled by drugs.

"Okay, what the hell!" I smile and put my arms out to him, surrendering my trust to him.

He slips the tab into his mouth, and then kisses me, placing it into my mouth with his tongue. I'm immediately aroused. As he pulls away, he looks into my eyes and smiles. I'm incredibly nervous and excited as I swallow it down. And then he tells me I owe him $20.

My only thought was *Shut up. You can't be serious.* I look at him, suddenly wondering who he is to be so rude. I stare into his eyes as I reach into my pocket to get the money I now owe him.

"Not here, later," he says as he turns back to the group.

"But you just said …"

He stops and turns back to me. "David, not here." He looks fiercely into my eyes.

I suddenly understand and let it go, but I'm not happy.

He then looks back to the group and says, "Let's go to the car."

They look around at each other, seemingly amazed by this ordinary statement, then look back at me, and finally at Seth. Without consideration of their drama, he grabs my hand and starts walking toward the parking lot. I look back as I'm being pulled away and notice a brief conversation happening among the group who watch us leaving. Then one by one, they follow.

We walk up to a red Audi A4 parked on the street several blocks from the club. It's an older one, probably a '97, but in good condition. Seth opens the driver door and climbs in. Black leather interior, I see. Richard and Peter follow me to the passenger side. Nice wheels. I offer to sit in back, but they both insist I take the front seat. They climb into the back, I sit in front, and the two doors slam shut behind us.

Seth smiles at me, then turns his head toward the back to look into the two faces staring back at him, then leans over and opens the glove box. He pulls out a small white leather bag. It's the kind of bag that you get when purchasing socks or underwear during the Christmas shopping season from some label like Tommy Hilfiger. He slides the zipper open and pulls out a small plastic bottle of clear liquid. Then he digs around and pulls out a much smaller brown glass vial. I throw my $20 into his lap. He stuffs it into his front pocket without comment.

"Ricky, pass me the Pepsi."

Ricky produces a half-full liter bottle of Pepsi with a small plastic cup placed over the top. Seth pours the clear liquid into the small brown vial, then pours that into the cup, adds a small amount of Pepsi, swishes it around and dumps it down his throat. He quivers from the horrid taste of the mixture. After his discomfort passes, he looks at me, excited.

"Ready?" he asks.

"What is that?"

"GHB. You'll love it."

"What's GHB?" I ask.

Peter shoves his head between the front seats. "Genius, don't ask, just drink. You are about to discover Heaven."

I look around into the eyes of everyone in the car. Their expressions seem to agree with his. I look back at Seth.

"It's okay, I promise," he says.

I look down at the cup, take a deep breath, close my eyes, and pour the strange fluid down my throat. I'm overcome by an instant burn and foul moldy taste. I gag as I swallow it down. "Oh God, this shit is horrible!" I yell, gasping for air.

Everyone laughs.

I continue to gag as I strain to keep it down.

"Gurl, in 20 minutes, you won't be saying that!" Seth says, followed with more laughter from the group. He smiles.

Then one by one, each performs the same ritual, though not as dramatically as mine. When Ricky finishes his, Seth looks at his watch and announces the time aloud for all to hear. Everyone then looks at his watch to confirm the time.

"What are you doing?" I ask, anxiously intrigued.

"Setting our G-clocks," Seth replies.

"G-clock. What's that?"

"If you take more than one shot in 90 minutes, you could fall out."

"Fall out? What does that mean?" I feel my monster becoming angry.

"Well, you get really out of it and occasionally you pass out."

"You pass out? You're not serious? Just pass out cold? What is this shit?"

Everyone starts laughing again. All right, the beast is here. I look at them wishing I could hurt them with my stare. I rest my glare on Seth. I'm guarded, frightened now.

"David, calm down. I would never hurt you."

"I don't know you. What is it, Seth?" I don't back down.

"It's GHB. It's no big deal. Don't worry. You're going to be fine." He then looks back at the group with a strained expression of "Help me."

I turn and stare out the passenger window. I begin to contemplate the consequences of my situation. Realizing I need to calm down, I shift my attention to the music. The music is the only thing that feels familiar. It helps to calm me.

We sit in the car for a while. I listen while they gossip about people and events I know nothing about. I sit quietly, worrying about what I've just done to myself.

"Well, are we ready to go back in?" Seth asks, looking into the rear view mirror at Ricky and Peter.

In one voice they both reply, "Yes." The doors open, we climb out of the car, and head back to the club. I walk alone.

Once inside, the group quickly disperses and Seth rushes up to me. He grabs my hand and turns to face me. "David, are you okay?" He looks sincere.

"I hope so," I reply. The fear in my stare is unavoidable. He leans his head a bit to the right in a gesture of empathy, as he empties his lungs and lowers his shoulders, deflating in the realization that I'm a little freaked out. He grabs my other hand, now holding both, and looks directly into my eyes. I see the pleading in his.

"David, I promise you I will never hurt you. Please know this about me. I need you to know that you can trust me. It's very important to me."

I watch his eyes and lips as he says this to me, looking for any sign of a lie. He looks back into my eyes and then puts his hands to my face, cupping my jaw. He pulls my face to his and begins to kiss me. It's a very long, deep, intense kiss. It feels so good. The drugs are peaking in my system now. I feel myself beginning to spin. I realize instantly that I am beginning to "roll" because of the rolling sensation the ecstasy is having on me. The energy seems to be pouring into the base of my spine and rolling up through my body like a warm fluid wave of energy. I'm breathing the music in through my lungs. The energy is within everything. It's everywhere.

The heat from Seth's hands launches a surge of sexual energy into my body. I look into his eyes, and a rush of energy begins to pour in through mine. Ecstasy and GHB. They are incredible together. And in this brief moment of time, I know what it feels like to not care what anyone in this world thinks about me. I have no fear; I have killed the monster. This pleasure is the only thing that exists. Pure, intoxicating, Ecstasy!

Seth leads me to the dance floor, chatting privately with several people along the way. As we return to the floor, I'm hit with waves that begin to overwhelm me. I'm spinning into a colorful wormhole. The music becomes distorted and tinny. I'm suddenly lost in my own mind, losing sight of the people around me.

"Holy shit!"

"What's wrong?" Seth asks.

"Nothing's wrong. I feel incredible!" The waves of energy are pouring throughout my body. I'm definitely rolling hard. He smiles, probably remembering his first time.

"Let's dance!" he says, then grabs my hands and pulls me to the middle of the dance floor. We step out and I immediately absorb myself into the beat and ride the waves. I surf the music for what feels like hours but is probably just one. The time passes like a fantasy visit to a dreamland. My body feels so good. A flow of endless possibility drifts through my mind. I suddenly understand everything. Everything I've ever experienced suddenly makes complete sense to me.

And then it evaporates as quickly as it arrives, former reality returning its obsessive stare. Wow, *that* was incredible!

This was my first journey to that place of nirvana, and when I arrived there, I understood entirely what the seduction was all about. I had never felt so incredibly warm and peaceful, music never resonated so beautifully within my soul, people were never so gorgeous, kisses tasted like chocolate, and the lust I felt for all of it was better than anything I had ever experienced. I had transcended the plane of this disconnected lonely reality and gone to a place where there was no fear, no pain, no ugliness, and no worry about tomorrow. In this destination of the gay universe, perfect nirvana had been achieved. This community of people had designed and built a world that made Disneyland look like a hula hoop. I felt completely alive for the first time in my life. It felt like Heaven.

As strange as the Universe can be, it turned out that Jeff had focused his attention on someone too. This was good; Jeff and I both had someone we wanted to be with, someone who wanted to be with us. And that helped us to both embark on this new journey. The passion, companionship, lust, and growing love provided both of us with a sense of adventure about life again. I think we both felt alive again.

I pass Dominic in the hall as he arrives to visit Jeff. "Hey Davey, how are you?"

"I'm fine, Dominic. Please stay out of my office."

A few seconds later, I hit the down button and look back at him as the elevator doors open. It's strange, he seems like a younger version of me, but with the confidence I never had. I watch as he slides his shiny new key into my doorknob. I hear the click of the lock and the door opens, and he glances back at me before stepping inside. He smiles that seductive smile. It feels good. I smile back as he closes the door behind him. What is it about him?

Over the next month, Seth and I spend a lot of time getting to know each other. Weeknights I'd get home from work and rush to finish my freelance projects, shower, pack an overnight bag, and head to his place. Weekends, we'd be out playing in the clubs.

I'd arrive at Seth's, climb into bed, and cuddle, as we'd talk each other to sleep, the way new lovers do. This happened more nights than not. At the time it seemed so romantic and innocent.

I'd awake mornings to find him standing over me, staring down through an aura of happiness. In any other life, in any other situation, there would be no doubting that he was looking at the love of his life, mentally pinching himself, wondering if it was really happening for him. And I would lie there, looking back at him, knowing it was true, at least for me.

Something about Those Little Pills

And so began my initiation into this world of new friends, dance clubs, drugs, sex, and sketch. *Sketch* is the slang term for anything weird you experience while high on drugs—someone behaving oddly, doing something socially unacceptable, or short-circuiting in a fit of odd behavior, brought on by the combination of getting too high, lots of drama, or witnessing something that was purely strange and unexplainable. It was also the term for the sunglasses some of us would wear at night while partying like rock stars, to cover the revealing eyes. All of this was known as *sketchy*.

Almost overnight, our weekends fell into a pattern that would usually start with Prefunk on Friday night. Prefunk was the getting together at any chosen pad to begin priming ourselves for the night's festivities. During these first weeks, it was usually at Ray or Heyden's place. At the Prefunk, everyone would be gathering, primping, laughing, and privately gossiping about whoever wasn't within earshot. Me, I'd do my best impression of psychedelic wallpaper.

Ecstasy, Crystal Meth, GHB, and Ketamine, known to this community of users as Ellen, Tina, Gina, and Kitty, were rampant. And believe me, when flying on this combination, *it was ecstasy*. Each bouncing body was a dancing pharmacy whose emotions and physical senses had been entirely possessed by pleasure gods.

Before heading out the door, we'd pop down a round of Ellen, and smoke, snort, or booty-bump some Tina. Booty-bumping involves Tina, water, a miniature turkey baster, and your bum hole. It was Seth's preferred method of delivery. Then we'd gulp down a quick shot of Gina and finish it off with a good bump of Kitty. After this, we'd pack our traveling pharmacy bag, throw one last glance in the mirror to be sure of our fabulousness, and head out to the clubs.

Arriving at the first club of the night was much like arriving at a Hollywood gala. When we walked in and filtered through the crowd, we were walking down the red carpet, all heads turning and everyone vying for a chance to introduce themselves. It seemed that my new group of friends knew everyone, and everyone wanted to be around them. Seth was always right by my side, like a good host. All night, he'd point out various people and give me a full Joan Rivers background. In no time I felt I knew everyone and *their story*. The bizarre combination of it all

19

intrigued me immensely. It was all so exciting and I really wanted to have some fun. And it was addictingly fun in the beginning. I had discovered what it was like to have buckets of hot, sexy friends, an incredible social life, a wonderful boyfriend, and lots of incredible sex. It was fantastically insane. *Seth, could you point out the cameras, please? Thanks!*

After a few hours at Neighbours, it was off to Contour for more dancing and mental gobbling of eye candy. Contour was a beautiful, dark, vibrating 100-year-old downtown brick netherworld, ebbing and flowing with progressive industrial music and a sexually molesting atmosphere, complete with sensual, olive-skinned, gold-glittered, black-eyed fire dancers. DJs poured orgasmic tribal beats through the air and into your spine as though magically connected by some unseen digital network. The warm sexual beauty in the air was palpable and sweet. It was a sophisticated, purposeful, yet drugged-out atmosphere.

I found myself surrounded by a world of amazingly sexy people who were drinking in a seductive, silent secret. Most were still feeling gorgeous, brooding, intelligent, and rebelliously perverse. Mingling and watching provided me with a taste of the invisible energy, and I tasted something naughty and secretive. When I attempted to pay attention to it, to put my finger on it, I'd be left with a strange penetrating nothing. But then I'd be quickly distracted by the people surrounding me and I'd be assimilated back into the energy and beat of this incredible physical state of presence, losing the morsel of what I was discovering. Except for the intently guarded electronic box in the corner of the dance floor, this was just another urban club. But in this box, and in the faces of those guarding it, and those of everyone under the spell of it, I saw a vision. And I knew this wasn't just another urban club. I didn't yet understand what it was, but I could see the effect it was having on my friends and others in the club. In his subtle way, Seth made sure I knew something very strange was going on.

After Contour, we'd head off to anyone's place for an In-Between. This was our time to regroup, change costumes, consume more party favors, and then head back out for the early morning clubs down in Pioneer Square, where the real action took place. By 6 am when Bananas opened, the drugs and 24 hours without sleep would be grooving together, creating a sublime condition that made this time and place feel like a destination somewhere else in the galaxy. The delirium and sketchiness that we'd all be feeling made these hours of the morning some of the most aberrant and memorable of those early times.

It is nearing the end of September. I'm entering the second month of this new life. Oh my God, I am so high right now. I'm outside. It is so beautiful. I'm leaning against Bananas. I'm captivated. The light turns red and the cars come to a stop. It's early, just past 8:00 am. The only cars passing our crazy corner are tourists and those arriving for the baseball game. Safeco Field is just two blocks away.

A silver Volvo wagon pulls up to the light. Immediately their windows begin to vibrate from the music pouring out of the club. They look over at our crazy corner. People are flowing out of the building and the sidewalk is as busy as the club inside. The door locks on the Volvo engage. Mom is driving. Everyone is staring at the craziness.

Suddenly, Fred roars out of the club, leaps up onto the concrete trashcan on the corner, jumps back down into the street and without warning, begins to perform for this frightened family. Mom freaks out, and in a fit of panic, she smashes down on the gas peddle and the car roars through the intersection, her family staring at us in horror. And the light is still red.

I nearly collapse in laughter, it is so funny. There aren't words to fully describe the insanity of it all. I can just imagine what normal people driving by in these morning hours think of our crazy corner. Bananas was a crazy, crazy place. I wish I had a video of it. The dance floor of Bananas was small, dark, and shoved into the corner, but all the energy was on that dance floor.

Now I'm bouncing away in my blissful dream, surrounded by Seth and the gang. The walls are rolling fantastically, appearing as translucent panels separating us from some nether world, combining with the music to open a doorway to another dimension. This is my first trip down the rabbit hole.

I reach through what seems like a black hole to grab Seth by the shoulders, not even recognizing the melted mess of this person I've come to know and trust. I pull him close, look him in the eye, and cry out "Baby, I think I am way too high."

Even though he has surpassed my consumption, with a profound look of absolute calm and control, he smiles back at me through his sketchy glasses, flashing that devious smile, and flips, "Gurl, you ain't high enough!"

With that, he turns back to the dance floor and bounces away. I stand there, stunned, wondering, "What the hell are you going to do now?"

Feeling surrounded, I turn in a big circle, visually swallowing everything around me. There is an energy, a presence wafting through the place, a force with a life of its own, hypnotizing everyone with a sexual pulse of ecstasy, somehow connecting everyone through the hypnotic beat of the drums and enveloping vocals.

Surprisingly, mixed in among the throngs of medicated partiers, each with its own galaxy of melding high and conversation, something else appears from the dark emptiness. The faces of people in suits, normal business people you'd not expect in such a crazy place. Couples in their 40s and 50s, people of class and stature, holding martini glasses, all watching me with a focused intent. Packs of them are scattered throughout the crowd. They are captivated, as if they are watching Cirque du Soleil perform, only in the secrecy of their basement, with strangers they know very well. Then I feel someone shaking me, trying to get my attention. I slowly look over my right shoulder at a woman. Her eyes are big. She is dancing around and holding my hand up to the sky, yelling out, "Can I get a witness! Somebody give me a witness!"

This was the beginning. These weekends of insane fun quickly became the norm of my life with Seth. And in the beginning, it all seemed relatively harmless. The initiation into his life of friends, clubs, drugs, and sex took me by surprise, secretly infiltrating my life. I had never experienced such a fascinating time. I never expected any of it.

Seth would put his arms around me and give me the king's tour of my fabulous new life by his side. His world was becoming mine. Each weekend was a new party with new places and new faces. I couldn't wait for Friday to arrive. The excitement of meeting so many people, getting all glam'd up, attending party after party with VIP status, falling in love with this man who appeared to be falling just as hard for me. Pinch me! The seduction of the whole package swept me off my feet like Cinderella at the Ball. For the first time, instead of just looking into the window at a life I had always dreamed of calling mine, longing for those beautiful, happy people to like me, love me, and welcome me in to play, I was on the inside, surrounded by them, looking back out at the world I had escaped.

Nature vs. Nurture

To try to better understand why everything happened the way it did, I have searched for answers in the life I have lived. What went so wrong that I could have unknowingly walked into darkness, and why was I so powerless to turn away? I am an intelligent, well-raised human being. Though my childhood was far from perfect, nothing in it seemed so horrible as to create such a powerful monster to shadow the rest of my life.

My growing up seemed normal to me. I'm an adopted, white, gay, lower-middle-class son of a Texas Cherokee mother and Mexican immigrant father. What? Okay, maybe this is unique. I was the baby of eight kids, with a substantial age gap between the rest and me. My adoptive mom birthed the first six of us. Much later she adopted me and then my older sister Becky many years after she adopted me. My dad adopted all eight of us. When they married, a week after meeting each other, Mom plus six kids, Dad didn't know a word of English and Mom spoke no Spanish. They met and fell in love one night while country-western dancing. Talk about love against all odds!

I had a pretty typical childhood. It was the 1970s in Denver. There was no cable TV, no Game Boys, no computers, or any of the rest of the technology of today. Nor were there fast food restaurants and malls on every corner. To eat at McDonald's was a great treat. It was a small, cozy little life we lived. My world was my family and the friends within my tight little neighborhood. We played with our Hot Wheels, Barbie dolls, bicycles, and Slip 'n Slides. We jumped on the trampoline, built forts and tree houses, and played in the creeks, fields, and broken-down cars around the neighborhood. It was a time when nobody locked their doors, kids could be outside after dark playing hide-and-seek, and we could walk to the Barn Store to exchange our coke bottles for a bag of penny candy, without any adults getting in our way.

My parents loved me more than any I could have hoped to have. Unconditional love defined. I was always by Mom's side, and was I ever a Momma's boy! Imagine a poor southern Baptist mother, devoting her life to her bazillion kids. Every dollar earned was happily spent on them, every minute thinking about them. She definitely lived for her children and she was a great mother.

Of the endless wonderful memories I have of her, there is one that captures so much of what I love about her. It was legal then to smoke in the grocery stores. There you'd find my mom roaming the isles of the market, with that strong presence she had, pulling two grocery carts, a cigarette with a two-inch ash dangling from her lips, and a big black beehive hairdo, pondering which 50 lb. package of ground beef to take home to the family. There you'd find me, happy as any kid could be, roaming the store, playing with everything foreign to me, and sneaking toys and candy into the basket whenever her eyes were turned away. It was such a beautiful, innocent time. All things considered, my childhood was pretty damn good. My mom was my best friend and she did a great job of raising me. My dad was a great father, too.

Growing up, I thought my childhood was normal. I believed my experiences and memories of those experiences were no different from what anyone else lived through during their childhood. Because I didn't know different, I didn't question any of it. Today, I know that much of it wasn't normal. There was a lot of dysfunction in my family. Some of my siblings and other relatives got into a lot of trouble and did some pretty bad things through the years. Some of it to me, but most of it just went on around me. My mom and dad did their best to shield me from it, but with so many kids and so much going on all the time, it was impossible for them to keep watch every second of the day. I don't think I need to share every sordid detail of it to make my point here. What is important is that I now understand that what I experienced then has affected everything that I've experienced since. It is an insight into understanding myself and the decisions I've made during my life, good and bad.

Until 7th grade, I was a pretty happy, outgoing little boy, in spite of my bad experiences. But that year, school stopped being my sanctuary and became a torture chamber. I lost all my friends, and everything that felt familiar to me evaporated in the heat of an unexpected fear. Mom decided it would be best for me to attend a junior high out of district. Kunsmiller, the school most of my friends were planning on attending, was known to be a very rough school. Several of my siblings went there and they got into endless trouble. My mom's experience with them and that school provided all the proof she needed to know she was making the correct decision for me.

Luckily, the father of my best friend Derek agreed with my mom, so with their blessings, we jumped district and attended Henry Junior High. But there was one problem with this situation. We had not a single class together, and I was completely alone for the first time. It was then that the overwhelming social fear I've struggled with began to show its face. That year I went from being a contented relatively well-adjusted kid with lots of friends to being paralyzed with fear. I couldn't make one friendship that meant anything to me. This crippling fear suddenly blindsided me. This probably was the year when my monster was born. Other than Derek, there is hardly a face that I remember from that year.

Well, I do remember one. Pamela Thomas. She rode on my bus, though we were never friends. She was a tough, bitchy, mean girl who loved to pick on the weaker kids, and I certainly was one of the weaker kids. I was very small and nerdy by most standards, as was Derek. One afternoon, as he and I were walking away from the bus, she spat out the window onto my head and proceeded to humiliate me in front of everyone. Seeing all the kids laughing and pointing as the bus drove away hurt more than what she had done. It was my first schoolyard humiliation.

When I look back on that year, seeing only flashes now of moments that I know were terribly frightening times for me, another piece of understanding falls into place. My memories of the anxiety and fear that drenched me then still sadden me today when I think about them. I've had a near lifelong struggle under this debilitating fear.

The summer following 7th grade brought an end to my friendship with Derek and again changed the course of my life. I suddenly knew what it felt like when the best friend of your life decides he doesn't want to know you anymore. We argued about something minor, not anything that was a friendship-killing event. From then on, he picked on me and tried to start fights with me any time we ran into each other in the neighborhood. We eventually got into a brawl when I grew tired of being humiliated by this person I never wanted to stop being friends with. He brought his friends and I brought my niece and sister, and everyone watched as I reluctantly beat the crap out of him. And then afterward, I asked him if we could be friends again. Though he said he'd think about it, we never talked again. But he never picked on me again either. When it came time to return to school that fall, I set my sight on another district's school. This pattern of flight became a coping mechanism that stayed with me. When I became frightened, I ran.

I stayed frightened in one way or another after that. I think it was then that I stopped trusting in relationships, and I think that made me want them even more. I longed to be surrounded by friends the way everyone at school seemed to be, but I was too shy to do much about it. I don't think I loved myself very much by then, probably blaming myself for being so different. I searched desperately for that love outside of me.

Suffering from social anxiety made this tough though. I expected rejection from everyone as inevitable. Yes, my monster was born. But I did manage to somehow find a best friend. And that often was enough to get me through, mostly because I was often falling in love with this one person.

Even today, I see it's just my nature to function better with a mate. I guess I have to admit that I'm not the hugely outgoing social butterfly I've always strived to be. I'm rather comfortable in a quiet, smaller world when I have a companion to share that world with, sexual or not. Back when I was painfully insecure, isolation and a small address book frightened the hell out of me. But when in love, none of that really mattered so much. Anytime I've been in love, I didn't need much else to feel happy. Love has always been a powerful mask to my insecurities.

With love as my springboard, I leapt from one boy to the next, a pattern that carried me into my adult life. When I was just 22, I met Jeff, and we have been in each other's lives ever since. Other than my mom, I had never known someone who reflected so much unconditional love. But even with such incredible love, life does what it will.

11.06.96

During a summer trip to Amsterdam, I developed what I believed to be nothing more than a blood blister on my sphincter, presumably from all the bike riding we had been doing. Bicycles are a big part of life in the land of the Dutch.

A few months after I returned home, my condition wasn't getting any better so I saw a doctor. Almost immediately he asked me if I'd ever been tested for HIV. I said no, and then proceeded to explain away why I had decided not to. Because Jeff and I were in a committed relationship, because we'd already engaged in unprotected sex together, we had chosen not to know. We didn't think we had it, and we didn't want to know in case we did. We believed the very knowing would prove detrimental to our health, with the negative thought patterns arising from the knowing, especially since there was no effective treatment or cure. We used all the excuses one creates to avoid facing fear.

Two weeks later we returned to the doc's office to get the results. When Jeff found out I had tested, he immediately went down and tested too. We sat in Dr. Elliott's office for what felt like an eternally long time, until finally he arrived. We were sure that he was going to tell us everything was fine, wish us a great life, and say goodbye. As he sat there at his desk and as the first tears fell from his eyes, I knew everything was not all right. Before the words left his mouth, I knew without a doubt that we were HIV+, and with that we would be soon be dead.

It was a typically wet, gray November day in Seattle, a day that forever changed what November means to us. We drove home quietly feeling the devastation of the news. We were told that my condition was much more serious than Jeff's. I had 109 t-cells remaining and a viral load of over 200,000. A healthy t-cell range is 800 to 1500. Because my condition was so serious, I was diagnosed with full-blown AIDS and immediately put on medication. I had to undergo surgery for my rump ailment, a condition known as a fistula. This can happen for a number of reasons, but it essentially is an infection originating in the digestive tract that creates an abnormal tract or passage to the body surface. Think of it as a wormhole next to the snake hole. Surgery would be required.

As if that wasn't enough, I had to begin taking an assortment of pills, known as the AIDS cocktail, to try to get my viral load under control. Luckily for me, and all of us fortunate enough to benefit from them, at the same moment that Jeff and I were diagnosed, like a blessing from God, new discoveries in the treatment of HIV/AIDS were emerging. Though I wouldn't realize it for several years, these discoveries would change the face of AIDS and dramatically affect our lives. We'd get to keep our lives. Most of us anyway. For too many, it hasn't been a magic pill, and for many others suffering throughout the world, they are too poor to get the medications. In all, too many people are continuing to die from this terrible virus.

As we drove home from the appointment, we hardly said a word to each other. Jeff drove and I just stared out the passenger window, watching the cold rain fall, wondering what it all meant. I was engulfed by profound loneliness; it was one of the darkest days of my life.

As soon as we arrived home, I disappeared into my bedroom closet of all places, where I privately fell apart, realizing I had just been given a death sentence. I felt the world was crushing in on me. I retreated to my closet for refuge. For a gay man, the closet has always been our protection. Though it was powerless to change the outcome, this was the only place I knew to go.

Surgery soon followed. Afterward, I lived a two-week misery of narcotics and horrific pain while my body recovered. It would seem that no pain pill could ease my suffering. I didn't want to be awake, because only when awake did I know what was really happening—on all levels. I didn't want to eat, because that meant my body would create waste, and eliminating that waste would cause more pain than I could handle.

I lost a lot of weight during those two weeks. I also lost a lot of what made David a happy boy. I went from being a bright beam of sunshine to the most depressed soul you've ever met. I was sure I was dying, and the pain and pills were there to remind me of it. No drug could help me escape or deny what I was dealing with. HIV-negative David died with that one sentence uttered by my doctor. And that death was as hard as any death I've ever experienced.

Just as soon as the healing of my rump had completed, I began my AIDS cocktail. Crixivan, AZT, and something else—I don't remember. It was an unbearable combination of chemicals that produced a condition that I can only describe as out-of-body experiences. I'd go numb from neck to waist and I felt that I wasn't connected to my body. I lived that hell for a couple of years or so. These drugs can be very toxic to the body, but when they are keeping you alive, you try not to complain too much. Headaches, gastrointestinal disorders, skin drying out like a sponge without water, it's hell. Too little water? Kidney stones. Not enough food or too much food with the pills? Headaches, taste disorders, and low absorption. If you miss a dose, you might become resistant and lose all benefit they provide. A hate-hate relationship bound by a marriage of necessity.

Not long after our lives were beginning to be spared by the drugs, the body changes began to appear, conditions known as lipodystrophy and lipoatrophy. Lipodystrophy is the condition characterized by abnormal or degenerative conditions of the body's fat tissue. Lipoatrophy is a subset of lipodystrophy, involving the loss of nearly all fat in the limbs and face, the subcutaneous fat. With lipodystrophy, one can also develop an increase in visceral fat, or gut fat, the fat deep within the torso. Sometimes they happen individually and other times together. Not only do you suffer what's happening inside your body, but there's outward trauma as well. As if suffering a horrifying death weren't enough to think about, we now had to suffer the humiliation of survival.

It's heartbreaking to me to know that some people feel justified and pleased at seeing this happen to another human being, just because that person loves someone differently than they do. It makes no sense to me. Why would any rational person want their friend or loved one, or anyone for that matter, to suffer such pain just for *loving*? Cancer, heart disease, MS, no other disease causes anyone to wish such horror on another. Why HIV and AIDS?

The immediate shame I felt from the scourge associated with HIV was overwhelming for me. I was afraid to tell anyone I loved, and I hated that I had to live with such a terrible secret. I needed support but couldn't reach out for it.

While sitting in a restaurant having dinner with Jeff several days after getting our results, I experienced my first public humiliation for having this virus, and the public had no idea that I was positive. As I sat there, looking around at all the other families eating and talking, I wondered what they would think if they knew I had AIDS. I imagined they would feel justified in humiliating me and attacking me. I imagined that if they did, they'd get away with it. I felt dirty for secretly exposing these people to me and my virus, even though I really hadn't. Because I knew what the world, and surely these people, thought about anyone who was a carrier of HIV, I had instantly accepted, with my diagnosis, a self-image of shame and disgust.

I'll never forget the sorrow I felt in that moment, as I looked down at the fork in front of me, wondering if they would let me use it had they known of my condition. Now I really hated being me.

A few weeks after my surgery, I flew home to visit my mother and family. Mom knew of my surgery, as did the rest of my family, but I hadn't yet shared the news of my diagnosis. I knew I had to tell her, but I also couldn't do it over the phone.

I did finally muster up the courage to tell her during that visit. She took the news quite well, though I'm sure she secretly mourned. She said she had always worried this might happen, as, I'd guess, does any parent of a gay man. But my mom loved me unconditionally, and this was more proof of that. I explained everything I had learned about the virus, treatments, and prognosis. My doctor had said almost immediately that with the new drugs, I would live a long life. This I repeated to my mom, even though I didn't yet believe it myself. Even if I didn't have much hope, I couldn't leave my mom without any. I did a good job of convincing her I would be fine. I just had to take my medicine and take good care of myself.

Together, we decided it would be best not to share this with the family. And it would be our secret for many years. I was fine with that because I feared they would look at me and treat me differently if they knew. I know it was hard for most of them to come to terms with me being gay, but that I didn't much care about. I was no longer ashamed of being gay. But having AIDS? That was completely different. HIV and AIDS was different back then. I was different back then. Our society today is so much more informed, though as a whole not nearly as informed as they should be. I felt I had no choice but to keep it a secret because I had no defense for an attack, should there be one.

In the weeks and months that followed, I did get better. My viral load dropped to undetectable within the first month and has remained there ever since. I regained the weight I'd lost from the surgery, plus some. With the rebounding of my immune system, my body was no longer fighting so hard and it showed in my weight and face. I would eventually look healthier than I had ever been before. Mentally though, I wasn't doing as well. It would take much more time to convince my mind that I wasn't going to die. Little did I know, it would be Mom who would be the first to leave.

April of 1998, I received a surprise call from my sister Donna. It had been a few weeks since my last talk with mom. When Donna called, I immediately knew something was wrong. Between sobs, she told me Flight for Life had just picked up Mom and they were headed to a hospital in Colorado Springs. She had had an aneurysm of the brain that had burst. With that sentence, my life again changed for the worse.

A year prior, Mom had started losing vision in her right eye. When she realized it wasn't getting better, she decided to see a doctor, who did some tests and realized that she had two locations of aneurysm, one of which was putting pressure on the optic nerve, causing the loss of sight. Though surgery was partly successful, they weren't able to repair the aneurysm near the optic nerve. They decided to come back at a later date. It was a day that would never come. In the blink of an eye, my mom was gone.

I wasn't ready to lose my mom, and the pain I experienced from that loss took a very long time to recover from. I grieved her death deeply, lamenting for days at a time. It was a loss that shook me to my core.

Many months later, peace finally came to me through a beautiful touch of grace. I was in bed, literally wailing, kicking, and screaming in pain, as often was the case during that time. My grieving wasn't pretty. For hours I cried and screamed at God, begging to be shown a sign that Mom was okay. For days, weeks, and months this same routine played out. On this night, magically, the lights in the room burst on. Startled, I sucked in a huge gulp of air and froze. In that moment, I knew without a doubt that my cries had been answered. That divine touch was a turning point in my grieving. After that night, I was able to finally feel ease from the pain and begin the process of letting her go. She had once told me, years earlier, that she would never hang around, haunting her family after she died. I know the intensity of my pain was the only reason she came to me. I needed to know she was okay. I needed to say goodbye.

After losing Mom, and with my physical and mental health stabilized, I soon became obsessed with achieving success. During the next several years, I worked endlessly on my career. We built a new house, I bought a new sports car, we traveled the world, and I shopped my ass off. I realized all of this was in my grasp again, or for the first time, and I was happy to have the chance to experience all of it. I still thought about time and figured it was short for me, but I wanted to experience as much of the finer things in life as I could. And in my quest for all of that, I was slowing creating a new unhappiness. I had chosen materialism to fulfill my end-of-life needs. But I didn't die, and materialism being what it is, the happiness from all of that faded rapidly, leaving in its wake loneliness, a lot of stuff to pay for, and an overflowing work schedule. If I wasn't bitching about being handcuffed to my computer working, I was crying about how empty I felt inside.

This was a very hard time for Jeff too. Not only was he dealing with his own mortality and quest for happiness, he had lost his ability to make me smile. Jeff has always been driven to bring happiness to my life and has been quite successful at it. It was heartbreaking for him to lose that.

On top of that, as I've said, our sexual compatibility was fading too. He understood this aspect of sexuality and wasn't as troubled by it as I was, but I developed a lot of resentment. I couldn't understand how something so important could just fade away. I'd never experienced this before, probably because I'd never had a long-lasting relationship before. And being so young, I couldn't imagine living life without sex.

Let's just say it wasn't much fun to be Jeff during those days. But he always managed to keep his calm, even when I was at my worst. When it seemed that things wouldn't get better, I started to consider that maybe it was time for us to make a change. There seemed to be just two choices; either we would sell the house and move to Capitol Hill, where we could surround ourselves with people *just like us* and have a chance at friends and renewed happiness, or I was going to move back to Denver to be close to my sister Sharon and my family.

Bud I didn't have to make the choice. Jeff came to me and said he wanted us to be together, that we'd make the move. I couldn't imagine my life without him. And in making that decision, hope bloomed and our familiar joyful selves returned for an encore.

Once we settled into our new home in the city, life became busy and exciting again. Living in the city, especially in Capitol Hill for us gay boys, changed everything. Just walking to the market became an adventure. In the city, people park their cars, if they even have one, and roam the neighborhood on foot. Restaurants, cafés, nightlife, parks, and being surrounded by people just like us brought excitement and interest back into our souls. On weekends, we'd walk a few blocks and shake our booties at the local gay bar. On beautiful afternoons, we'd jump on our bikes and ride to the park and have a picnic among all the other gay couples. The difference from our isolated suburban life was like night and day. We felt connected again, part of something, surrounded by members of our tribe. It didn't take long until we were making friends and socializing. It seemed as though all of our troubles had been left behind. But it didn't last, and soon enough I found Internet dating and Seth.

I Have a Secret

Within weeks of welcoming Seth and his world into mine, I began to notice that something didn't seem quite right, like a wrinkle in time or a dream with things impossibly out of place. Even when we weren't doing drugs, what I began to notice didn't make sense. My boyfriend and his associates slowly started to reveal a side of themselves that I hadn't noticed in the beginning. The longer I shared their experience, the more I grew to know about them, and the more I realized they shared secrets that only those who got close to them could discover.

Even though Ray was close to Seth, he always made me uneasy: something about the way he looked at me, how he always kept me at a distance, how he avoided befriending me for as long as he could. Initially, I wondered if he was jealous of Seth and me or if he didn't approve. I had dealt with a jealous friend before, so that in itself didn't frighten me too much, though rejection always did hurt.

"Ray, have you seen Seth?" I ask.

"No. I thought he was with you." He looks around, locks eyes with Richard, and nods. Richard registers his communication, searches around, and then heads off.

"Did he say anything to you?" I ask, pretending not to notice what has just taken place. "I don't understand why he would just disappear."

"I don't know. You have to ask him," Ray flips as he too studies the surroundings before walking away. A few moments later, Seth returns.

"Hey baby, what's wrong?" he asks.

"Did I say something was wrong?"

"No, but you have that look. Come on, David, what's going through that head of yours?"

"What look? Oh, the one of 'Hmm, I wonder why my boyfriend has been MIA for over an hour'?"

"I was right over there, talking to Fred."

"I talked to Fred. He didn't know where you were."

"Then I must have been with John."

"But you just said you were with Fred."

"I talked with John before Fred."

"Oh, okay Seth, I see. Well, I'm leaving. You have a great night." I turn away and head to the entrance. He chases after me.

"David, stop!" He pulls my shoulder. I stop and turn to him.

"No, Seth, I won't. I'm leaving." I glare into his eyes for a moment, then turn and walk away. I sense he is watching me walk out the door. He doesn't try to stop me. Perfect! I storm to my car, growing angrier at each step. As I open the door, I feel a soft, warm hand upon my neck. I spin around, wrap my hands around his head, pull his mouth to mine and kiss him with everything inside me. *Shit, what am I doing?*

"I'll call you tomorrow. Be good." I jump into my car, the engine roars to life, I back out and drive away. I race home, park, take the stairs to the fifth floor, and quietly let myself in. I tiptoe to the bathroom to brush my teeth and wash my face. I pop a couple of Tylenol PM with my meds, grab a pillow and head to the living room. I lie down on the couch, pull the throw around me and fall asleep as quickly as I can. I just want this night to be over.

It was after this night that I began to pay close attention to the behavior of Seth and his friends. The way they looked at me with such contempt, when they didn't think I was noticing. Mostly it was his friends doing this, but in time he did too. When they sensed I had noticed something, they would smile and wrap their arms around me, an attempt to pull me in like a new best friend, thinking it would make me forget what I'd seen. And for a while it did.

At first I thought, "Okay, Dave, maybe this is just you being nervous." But I knew it was more than that, I just didn't realize how much more. Unfortunately I had a secret of my own, and that was clouding my reasoning, my ability to understand. Whenever I sensed trouble coming from my new world of friends, I ended up blaming myself for it. I wondered if they somehow knew what I had yet to reveal.

Seth didn't know my HIV status. I hadn't put him at any risk, because we always had safe sex, but I knew he needed to know this about his boyfriend, to decide for himself if he wanted to have a relationship with someone who was HIV+. I used to believe that if someone wanted to know, they would ask. But nobody ever asked. That's why I have come to the conclusion that we should always tell.

With each passing week, my anxiety grew. The more I worried about the secret I was keeping, the more I associated the bizarre behavior of Seth and the gang with it. I couldn't believe I had let so much time pass without dealing with this. I never meant to. I had built up so much fear; it felt impossible to confront it. A lifetime of low self-esteem ensured that assertiveness was a slippery slope for me, especially with this. Somehow I could never get the words out or find the right moment to do what needed to be done. But one strange evening changed all that.

"What do you think of the E?" Seth asks.

"It's really strong, baby." I'm intense, serious, and a little frightened.

"It's supposed to be ecstasy, mister, not agony!" He smiles, rolls his eyes, and tugs at the back of my hair, then looks around the club. He seems to be looking for an escape. I attempt to follow his attention, but he notices and turns back to me.

"Everyone's going outside. Do you want to come with us?"

"Yea, I do. Is it okay? It seems like everyone is distant tonight."

He sighs, "They're just high. Come on." He turns and walks away. He doesn't take my hand. He always takes my hand. He always walks with me.

By now, I understand how my emotional senses grow very strong on Ecstasy, seeming even clairvoyant at times. It can be overwhelming, becoming all I can think about. I pick up on things that play out correctly, things I know nothing about until they happen. I wonder if it's just a magical effect of the drug, one that everyone experiences. Tonight, Seth and his friends don't seem comfortable with me. I can't tell if I'm discovering something about them or if they are discovering something about me. This night something is definitely happening. Everyone is so intense; the energy is very dark and heavy. And not one soul is engaging me; I am the odd one out.

On our way back to the front entrance, I decide to make a side trip to the restroom, to pull myself together. Seth doesn't even notice that I'm not behind him. This saddens me.

The bathroom is empty. I walk to one of the two sinks in the corner, across from the urinals. I turn on the water and stare into the mirror at myself. *What's wrong with you?* I splash cold water on my face and continue to stare into my eyes, looking for anything to help me. A group of boys roar into the bathroom, shaking me from my private moment. I dry my face and hands, and then head back out to find everyone.

Outside, I see the group gathered near the steps, their backs turned toward me. Feeling uncomfortable, unwanted, I stop and look for another place to go. I step back into the shadows and watch. I'm following the group because we had all arrived together, not because anyone is making me feel my company is wanted.

All of a sudden, Ray dramatically appears, pulls Seth aside, and whispers something in his ear. Seth yells "NO!" and starts crying. In that instant, I know that my secret has been discovered, taking with it my last opportunity to right this wrong with any honor. I know it is over and time for me to go. I turn, tears welling up in my eyes and blindly make my way down the stairs to my car, open the door, fall into the driver's seat, and lock the doors before melting in heartbreak. I wipe my eyes, take a deep breath, and start the car.

I quickly pull out of the lot and speed away, hurrying to the safety of my home with Jeff. Along the way I struggle to keep from falling apart. I turn down my street and push the button and the aluminum gate begins to rise. I drive in and slip into my stall. I feel numb now; I can no longer cry. I just sense something really bad is happening.

As I walk to the elevator, I hear people outside the gate. They are very heated about something. I recognize the voices; I realize it's them.

"Let's fucking kill him!" I hear someone say.

"Mitch, shut the fuck up!" That sounds like Seth!

I panic and run the other way, bypassing the elevator and head up the stairs. In my apartment, I wake Jeff and tell him what happened. He is instantly concerned and wraps his arms around me, pulling me in, comforting me the way a mother would a child. We talk for a while; he calms me as much as he can, and then we climb into bed together. There will be no sleeping for me.

Early the next morning, Jeff leaves for work and I just lie low. My cell phone keeps ringing. It's Seth, so I turn it off. I can't imagine what he is going to say to me. By early afternoon, the Ecstasy has worn off and I am much calmer, so I decide to listen to my messages. To my surprise, Seth doesn't seem mad at all. Just perplexed at why I had left. *What the hell? Had I been completely wrong about the night before? How could he not be mad at me? And what about the things I had heard outside the gate?* Now I am perplexed. I know I have to call him.

When he answers, it is more of the same. "Why did you leave? Where did you go? I was so worried!" He says he stood outside my building all night calling my name, trying to get me to come out. I never heard it, but maybe he did. I am too stunned to say much of anything, so he asks me to come over so we can talk in person. The idea of going over there frightens me. Maybe this is a setup, just to get me over there. I pace and puzzle over it, eventually deciding that it is safe, that I should go. I know it is now or never—I have to tell him the truth, whatever the outcome.

When I arrive there, I can tell he is still flying high, but he seems relatively calm. We talk about what happened, how uncomfortable I had felt all night.

Apparently, Ray had told him that a drug dealer friend of theirs had gotten busted, and I witnessed his reaction to the news. His reaction didn't seem appropriate. He didn't seem that close to anyone in his world, enough to bring him to tears, but I accept it as truth. Why would he lie? It is all so weird.

I walk over to the window and stare out at the courtyard for what feels like an eternity. Seth is sitting on the edge of his bed, quietly watching.

"There's something you need to know about me," I say.

He pats the bed next to him, signaling me to join him. I slowly walk over and sit down. I stare into his eyes for a while, aching to move my lips to speak, but then look away in frustration. Each time I attempt to open my mouth and begin the hardest sentence of my life, there is only silence. I look back at him and we lock eyes.

"You're going to hate me when I tell you this."

He just watches me with a strange, expectant calm. *God, please help me.* I continue to sit there unable to speak.

"David, this is getting weird. What is it?"

That did it. Afraid of being weird, I find the courage I need, I sit up, look him in the eyes, and say the nine syllables, "Seth, I am HIV+."

Without skipping a beat, he replies, "So?"

"Seth, I have HIV and I didn't tell you. How can you not be upset?"

"I never asked. We've had safe sex. What's the problem?"

"I thought you'd be angry. I thought you'd break up with me."

"Why should I be angry?"

"Seth, you should be really upset right now. How can this be so easy for you?"

"It's not easy for me. I just found out my boyfriend has HIV. Why didn't you tell me sooner?" he asks.

As pathetically wrong as it sounds, I explain how one day became the next and my wall of fear grew and grew. I don't have an answer except fear. We talk about that for a while. Ironically, Seth is very good at helping me see my fears as just fears, encouraging me to gain strength over them. In this moment he does just that. He helps me to forgive myself for this indefensible breach of trust, to realize I am human, that he loves me, and that we will be okay.

As soon as this is dealt with, he calls Ray, stepping out of earshot for the short conversation. I attempt to get closer to listen, but he watches my every move and prevents me from hearing anything. Ray arrives a few minutes later and welcomes me back with an eagerness that is unusual for him. It unnerves me. We then have a breakfast of EKG, and the weekend's festivities continue.

It's Him or Me

My relationship with Seth was intense and quickly complex. That combination worked to create a relationship like none I had ever known. The attraction and attention he focused on me felt genuine and deep. To this day, I can't decide if his love for me was true. I want to believe it was. I guess that wanting to believe is what kept me engaged for so long.

Over the next couple of months, our relationship seemed to shift into a new phase. Not as carefree and innocent as it had been before, but not necessarily bad either. My home life with Jeff, however, was taking a turn for the worse. Dominic began to spend a lot of time there. When I was home, I felt very uncomfortable, like a third wheel or an unplanned guest at what was supposed to be a cozy romantic night home for two, sans me. "Oh, we didn't realize you'd be here tonight," they'd say.

I'd retreat to my office to do some work while they were making themselves dinner, giggling and cuddling in the living room. At times it felt too awkward to leave my office at all. I would usually get too upset to get any work done, so I'd angrily pack a bag and head out the door. It wasn't so much that I felt what they were doing was wrong. We were both dating other people. But because it was in my face, where I lived, that made it hard to endure.

In fact, it didn't take long for me to realize that it was time for Jeff and me to take the next logical step and separate. Living together no longer worked or made any sense for either of us.

Seth was all for this, and he encouraged me to do it immediately.

"I don't think it's healthy for either of you. You both need to let go and move on."

"Jeff and I've been friends for 11 years. It's not that easy."

"I won't have him in my life, David. I want you, not him. You need to decide who you want."

"Are you giving me an ultimatum? Jeff is always going to be my friend, Seth."

To get his way, Seth could be down right cruel in his forcefulness. It was his method of manipulation over me, and it worked very well. I suspect I would have been an easy target for anyone like him back then. My need to be liked was much stronger than my ability to say no.

I've always enjoyed treating others. I'm a generous person and I find great pleasure in being so. Seth had a limited income as a retail clerk. Almost immediately I paid for everything he and I did together. When his car broke down, I paid to fix it. I did it because I knew he needed to get to work. When he needed money to cover his rent or to put food in his cabinets, I provided. I loved him; I didn't want him to hurt. Dinner out, night at the movies, cover charges and certainly all drugs we consumed—I paid for all of it. And foolishly, I spared no expense. Thousands and thousands of dollars I spent this way. I went through my entire savings and maxed out my credit in the year we were together. I was a fool in love.

Seth made every excuse to avoid paying for anything, mostly playing the sympathy card, a dependable technique in those days. At coyly perfect times, he and his friends would slip up and refer to me as Sugar Daddy. I say "coyly" because they managed to do it in a way that made me appear insecure and awkward if I did anything but laugh at the "joke." I was quite insecure then, so I guess that made it all the easier. During our whole time together, Seth bought me one $15 housewarming gift when I moved into my apartment. Ah, sweet love …

After our breakup talk, Jeff and I hugged each other and cried together. We never lost respect for each other and our friendship. It was that friendship that would play a lifesaving role later on.

Seth and Ray worked with extreme fervor to get me to sever my ties with Jeff. In the beginning, I didn't understand why, and many times I considered the misleading ideas they poured into my mind. But to their continual frustration, I always concluded that Jeff's love and devotion to me were genuine. His honesty has always come through.

The following weekend I walked the neighborhood in search of a new place to call home. It was surprisingly fun. This area had always held a special place in my heart. Capitol Hill is an eclectic little neighborhood just steps from downtown Seattle. Before the hell I went through, I thought it was a place of wonderfully diverse people, fabulous restaurants, boutiques, coffee houses, and an exciting nightlife catering to every taste. But that changed almost overnight for me. I suppose the dark underworld that took over my life had been present there long before I arrived, but the Hill felt noticeably decayed by the time I moved away. The energy permeating every alleyway and corner seemed to give testament to the sinister dealings that hid behind many a closed door and pulled curtains. A friend of mine recently spoke of Capitol Hill as a Babylon of our age. It was another heartbreak for me to turn on the Hill as it had turned on me.

I Begin to Wonder

In no time I found a great little one-bedroom apartment in a new building, just a few blocks from where I had been living with Jeff. Seth and I pondered living together, but we felt it was too soon and we decided against it.

Seth and Ray were there to help on moving day, so Jeff did his best to stay away, undoubtedly to hide his own emotional breakdown. As soon as we arrived and started filling boxes, I was knocked off my feet by my own gale-force emotions. Over 11 years of sharing my life with Jeff was coming to an end, something I had never believed would really happen. All of a sudden nothing made sense to me. I wondered where we had gone so wrong. I wanted to close my eyes, cover my ears, and wish it all away. It was all happening too fast.

"Maybe you can dry your eyes long enough to help load the elevator," Seth says. He is suddenly cold and distant. My monster roars to life.

"What? Did you think this would be easy for me, Seth?"

"And you think it is for me?"

"It should be. I'm leaving Jeff to be with you. I think you'd be pretty damn happy, actually." I bend over to grab the two boxes stacked at the front door.

"Why don't you just stay with him if this makes you so sad?"

I stop, rise up, and glare at him.

"Maybe I should."

Returning from the elevator, Ray opens the door, hitting me with it accidentally. Sensing the anger between Seth and me, he says, "I'm going to take this load down to the truck." He grabs the two boxes by my feet, looks at Seth, then quickly turns and leaves.

"What is wrong with you? Why are you being so mean to me?" I say, while reaching out with my left hand to slam the door behind Ray. My eyes never leave Seth's.

"Maybe you should think about me right now. Seeing you so upset about leaving him doesn't make me feel very good."

"No, Seth, maybe you should think about *me* right now. This isn't about you. This is about *me*. So let's just move *my* shit out of here, into *my* new apartment, and deal with the rest of *this* shit later. Can we do that?"

"Fine." He pushes past me, opens the door, and slams it behind him.

I couldn't believe what was happening. As we continued to move, I thought about everything that had happened, wondering if I was making a big mistake. Realizing my reaction was stronger than he'd planned for, he did his best to stay out of my way. I wanted to break down and cry, but instead I shoved my emotions into the boxes with the rest of my belongings, and hardly spoke a word for the rest of the day.

After the moving was done, I settled into my new home, finding some unexpected joy in living alone. It didn't last long though. Seth and I were together all the time. Life did grow happier again after the move. Playing house together took our relationship to a deeper level. I have always been the nesting type, so this helped reinforce a strong bond between us. It didn't much matter what we were doing; decorating our little urban box, grocery shopping, cooking dinners, cuddling on the couch watching movies, spooning and napping on rainy afternoons, or dreaming about the future together. As bad as our arguing could get, it could be just as wonderful between us.

"Wow, what is that smell?" I ask. It's been a long day at work. I drop my messenger bag, hang my jacket, and then follow my nose into the kitchen.

"Spaghetti." He smiles as he tastes the sauce.

"Yum." We wrap our arms around each other and kiss.

There was always so much affection between us, more than I ever experienced in a relationship. It was intoxicating. Weeknights, after dinner, we'd curl up on the couch together and watch television. He'd pull the throw up over our feet and tuck us in. Night after night, we'd quietly fall asleep together, hardly ever watching a complete program. And that's all I needed to fall in love. I fell deeper and deeper with each passing night.

My swanky new digs at once became the pre-funk location of choice, probably because it was an exceptionally nice place to hang. Leeches seem to like beauty, especially if they aren't paying for it.

I went very modern industrial with that place. Black leather, brushed steel and glass furniture and charcoal grey accent walls. I love to decorate, and that apartment was so much fun to decorate. Seth really loved to show it off to his friends.

"Damn, girl, what a great pad!" Matthew says.

Seth smiles and replies, "Matt, you should have seen us shopping for this place. We bought everything in one day and loaded it all into his car. It was crazy, I was buried under shopping bags on the way home."

I purchased nearly everything new when I moved into that place because I couldn't bear the thought of Jeff reaching for something that wasn't there, reminding him that I wasn't either. I could see him hurting in that moment, the way you might when someone you love has died. Just thinking about it made my heart hurt, so I took as little as possible when I left.

It didn't take long for my relationship with Seth to become strained again. We returned to arguing a lot, mostly on the weekends when we were partying. It was usually jealousy that started the fighting, as it had been from the beginning. I'm sure the drugs didn't help. As the newness of us started wearing off, so too continued the dissolving of the illusion he had created for me, slowly revealing the truth of this new world I was becoming part of. The drugs, the drug dealers, the sketchiness, and the sex, it was all engulfing my life. Like peeling off little pieces of wallpaper, these were my first glimpses of a much larger story that I had yet to uncover. But I was falling in love, and that superseded everything that was wrong with my life.

Unlike the Seth I had grown to know and love, this other Seth was becoming very flirty and distracted. When we were out, he seemed much more interested in the other boys. Instead of staring lovingly into my eyes, he'd keep his back toward me, literally positioning himself so that I couldn't see his face. I grew annoyed with the peculiar way he worked to keep me behind him as he patrolled the club, seemingly on some mission. Unable to see his face, I started looking around with him, looking at what he saw, to try and understand this irritating habit of his. It was then that I noticed he wasn't just looking away from me, he was completely engaged in something else. Watching the way he scanned around obsessively, I could suddenly see why he had no time to look at me. Many things fell into place in that moment. Those many moments of bewilderment when I couldn't understand what was happening now started to make some sense.

The day I discovered there was a stranger in my life, the last of our innocence forever evaporated. Upon this realization, his drifting became so painfully obvious, I wondered how I had ever missed it. When he'd lock onto a guy, it was as though they were having a conversation telepathically. You'd swear one knew exactly what the other was thinking. This went way beyond any cruising I had ever experienced. He'd go from guy to guy, one to the next, evening after evening. Sometimes he'd get interested in a particular guy, cunningly positioning himself, and us, in view of his prey most of the night. It was this that we started arguing about. And it was this that opened a window for me to begin seeing his method of lying to me. He never stopped engaging in this type of cruising, he just got more careful in the way he did it. In time, he started pulling disappearing acts, undoubtedly to get out of my sight. I'd pathetically crawl the club looking for him, with his friends surely watching in amusement, only to have him swear he was just standing *over there*. Many times I'd see him talking to someone he had been *looking at* and amazingly on cue, Ray or someone would show up and pull me away. It was as though everyone understood what was going on, everyone except for me.

It didn't take long until I became visibly upset. My senses knew I was being made a fool of, no matter what he had to say about it. Whenever he realized I was approaching my breaking point, he'd switch gears and come back to me, pouring on the love and concern. We'd go outside to cool off and talk. He'd say so intently playful, "What's wrong, David? I see that look in your eyes. What's happening in that little mind of yours?"

"Seth, I know what's going on. I may be high right now, but I am not a fool."

"What are you talking about, David?"

"Where have you been, Seth?"

"I just went to the bathroom."

"You were gone for over an hour."

"I was?"

"Yea, you were."

"Oh yea, Heyden called me out to his car for a bump of Kitty. He took forever. You know how messy he is when he is high."

"Matthew said Heyden told him that he needed to run home for something. He saw you and two other boys get into *your* car and drive away."

"Heyden needed to get more pills. We were gone 10 minutes at the most."

"Fuck this, I'm going home."

"David, don't do this. We're doing so good."

"Yea, and you just blew it. I'm leaving. Goodbye, Seth."

Whenever my anger couldn't be calmed with a little heart-to-heart, he would shift into damage control, once again becoming the perfect boyfriend. He could psychoanalyze me like no one else I've known. He always found some underlying cause to my fears, and he used it to twist the situation back into his control. He and Ray were masters at this.

This was the pattern of our arguing. Every weekend this routine would take place, so much so that our friends could see it coming and start planning around it. Anyone who arrived with us would get what he needed from the car and start searching for other transportation. One by one they'd make the rounds of sad looks, hugs, and mocking sympathy before ditching us for less drama. Then would begin my Seth-controlled therapy sessions.

Initially they were successful, and we'd return to hugs and kisses from everyone, a hero's salute to Seth, and rounds to the car to replete our diminishing drug levels. Once I had been talked down, the cycle would begin again, another episode of *The Seth and David Show*, Season 1. From the many revelers that eagerly surrounded us, I'd guess our ratings were huge. What had been unknown and unbelievable to me suddenly became the conditions of my life. I was now trapped by my heart into a life that was much different from the one that I had been sold on. For better or worse, I was deeply in love with Seth now. I had trusted him when he said he wouldn't hurt me. And now that he was hurting me, my heart kept searching for proof that it wasn't true. He knew I was doing this, and he knew how to give my heart what it needed to stay.

It was during our pre-funks, after opening my door to anyone Seth's group invited in, that I started to notice the strange things happening in my new world. Although we were doing many drugs, my memories aren't worthless. I wasn't living in a drunken stupor of alcohol or in the numbing blur of cocaine or heroine. Take the blue pill and the story ends. The drugs these people preferred had me wide-awake and fully aware of what was happening. Take the red pill and you see how far the rabbit hole goes. They only had red pills.

So often, people would disappear into the bathroom for reasons unknown but curious to me. It was a revolving door when certain people were visiting, including those of our inner circle. I knew it wasn't to do drugs because we were all doing them openly. Nor was it even to step beyond the limits of our intake because the only avenue left was intravenous, and I knew this wasn't happening. My new friends seemed to have a prejudice against doing that and I had never seen any evidence of it, with them or Seth. Believe me, I suspected it, and looked for it. Growing up, I discovered that a brother and sister of mine were injecting drugs, so I became familiar with the signs. They didn't exist here. This secret was something different.

One night, a larger, more varied group than normal was visiting. For the first time, I felt like there were some truly bad people in my house. And on this night, I was exposed to something I didn't expect. Everyone was sitting around enjoying the music, rolling in their high, and preparing to depart for the clubs. The usual rounds to the bathroom were playing themselves out, as well as various intimate conversations that seemed to get quieter as I passed, paired with that look I had become so familiar with. It was a look I could best describe as one of naughty pleasurable disdain. Needless to say, this made it a bit awkward to invite myself into the conversations. In my own house no less.

By chance, I unexpectedly walked in on Seth and Ray in the bathroom. They were both huddled under the sink, focused on some task. It looked like they had lifted out the floor of the sink cabinet and were focused on something within.

They quickly slammed the door in my face. Later, Seth acted distant and odd, specifically avoiding my stare, something I had now come to know so well. I parked myself near the kitchen and just watched.

"Why doesn't your boyfriend know?" Thom says to Seth. Seth whispers something into his ear. Thom looks surprised.

"Oh shit," he says. He realizes I'm watching them, trying to figure out what's happening. Seth sees me and turns away. Thom stares at me, trying to understand something and then turns his attention away. From then on Thom kept much more distance between himself and me. He went from what I thought was a possible friend to just a face in that purposely distant crowd. In the beginning, everyone in that crowd had their hands all over me. In time, everyone kept a noticeable distance.

Also as time progressed, my curiosity about the mysteries I was being kept from grew stronger. Instead of brushing off their odd and secretive behavior with bruised anger as I had been doing, I began to take notes. Even in the most obscure moments, this little reporter was taking mental snapshots and processing data. At home alone with Seth mid-week or observing the activity in the bathroom at the clubs, and every moment in-between, I was paying very close attention. In doing so, I learned many things about my sketchy new world.

At home I began to see that Seth had a secret I initially thought was another man. It turned out to be something I could have never imagined. In the outside world, I learned that the owners of one of the clubs we played at had been busted videotaping boys without their knowledge. Hidden cameras in the bathrooms, at crotch-level. Initially it was assumed they were just perverts sneaking a look, but with the developments of my secret investigating, I was sure they were on the same fact-finding mission I was. Only illegally, with hidden cameras. I recognized the value that doing this could provide, but I never found the courage, or stupidity, to break the laws to do it. I think I was the only person whose morals got in his way in this scene.

Something odd was taking place with these people. Ironically, evidence of their truth was right in front of my face, etched on the mirror in the bathroom of Arena, a club Seth was particularly fond of and where I witnessed some of the most bizarre and revealing behavior. It was there I came to know some important faces that would play a later role in what should have been my last night on this earth. This was also where Mass took place. Mass was a traveling circuit party event that happened on Sundays, where boys high on ecstasy partied heavily under an almost religious devotion before heading off to various secret sex parties, common in this scene. Seth invited me once, then never again.

Over the years, Arena struggled to find a consistent audience, reopening many times under different names. During one particular flavor, when they were playing host to Sunday Tea Dances, I journeyed to the men's room to find a member of our outer circle getting sketchy in a stall. He was groaning in pain and flailing into the privacy walls of the commode. It looked like he was being thrown around like a rag doll, but he was alone in the stall. It was disturbing to witness. As I listened to him groan and smash into the walls, I glanced over at the mirror and read, "It's what's inside that matters" etched into the glass above each sink. By then, I was beginning to understand what cleverly masked signs like this meant. I realized this wasn't the simple bit of wisdom that most would interpret it to be. I knew it was literally referring to something inside these people who were now part of my life. I just didn't know what it was. But I was beginning to realize that so much of this truth had probably always been hiding in plain sight, just like this message in the mirror. If you know to look for it, this truth is everywhere. But you wouldn't even know to look for it unless you'd been exposed to it. A forbidden sexual secret. Now I just had to figure out what it was.

As my relationship with Seth progressed, so did my friendships with the rest of the cast, not only within our inner circle, but also in the many faces beyond. An important part of this story includes the larger scene. As my frustrations with Seth grew, I began to get feedback from the others about this crazy situation I was part of. Initially Matthew was the first to reach out to me. Matthew argued a lot with his partner Heyden, much like the way Seth and I did. Recognizing each other's pain, we started leaning on each other for support. It was obvious to me why Matthew was having problems with Heyden; it should have been obvious why we shared similar hurts.

It was no secret that Heyden seduced any and all boys he could get his hands on with his drug dealings. No secret to anyone but Matthew. After some time, it was apparent to me that nobody else was going to share this fact with him, so I did. I couldn't sit by and watch Heyden make a complete fool of Matt, even though everyone else kept silent. In gratitude, Matthew provided some insight into my situation. In one sobering telephone conversation, his strong advice to me was, "David, these are some really fucked-up people you are mixed up with. Be very careful." When I asked what that meant, he wouldn't go into much detail, especially when it came to Seth. Nobody ever said much about Seth. Was it out of allegiance or fear? I don't know.

My biggest frustration through this time was how nobody would help me understand what was happening to me. It seemed as though everyone had already sold his soul and was bound to that contract. What was this secret that was making everyone silently watch my story unfold?

One Saturday night, I was home and Seth was out playing, an arrangement that was becoming typical. It became normal for him to be without me, especially after he'd been awake for 2 to 3 days. The sketchier he was, the less he wanted my company. On this night, I had become frightened by the atmosphere at the club and decided to return home. Later, he called to check in on me. By then, I was becoming very cynical of his motives. By then, I had many reasons to. He said he was going to stop in and say hi. Because I loved him, I welcomed this offer to put me first. I was getting used to his public frustration of me, but I still longed for him to be with me.

When he arrived, he was higher than I had ever seen him, his energy unusually excited and strange. There was an uncontrolled sexual energy emanating from him, something much stronger than any effect of Ecstasy or other drug combinations I'd ever seen. It was my first time witnessing this indicative tell-tale look of secret pleasure and I wouldn't come to understand it until much later. He begged me to come with him, saying he and Heyden were on a break from the club, heading back to Heyden's place to replenish their drug levels. He begged and pleaded with me to join him. I sensed it wasn't because of any genuine desire to have me by his side, but more out of desperation for me to witness something. He seemed to need me to go with him, like my being there was important somehow. This alarmed me, and I knew I shouldn't join them. Ultimately failing to convince me, he stormed out the door. A few minutes later I called him to talk about what was happening. I was in no way prepared for what happened next.

There is no mistaking the sound of sex. The breathing and moaning one makes in the heights of passion. Even through the phone, there is no hiding those sounds. When Seth answered his phone, this is what I heard. I could also hear the engine revving as whoever was driving shifted through the gears. I heard this in my ear and out my window too. Heyden lived just a few blocks from my apartment, so I could hear them driving up the street. I listened in shock. No doubt about it, Seth was having sex, in the car, with me on the phone. He attempted to pass it off as nothing but eventually he lost control of himself and dropped the phone. I listened for a few minutes to the moanings of what sounded like several people, and after screaming his name over and over, I hung up, horrified and heartbroken.

With this, my jealousy exploded. I started looking for any signs that Seth was messing around. After catching him chatting in the sex rooms we met in, it became hard to deny that something might be going on. He had some dumb excuse about the chatting making him feel better about himself and that I had nothing to worry about, he'd never hook up with anyone. He even suggested we seek couples counseling to help with my insecurities. He was incredibly skilled at turning the cards on me, convincing me that his love for me was true. He got me to see that I was causing all of our problems out of some irrational fear. He insisted that he was deeply in love with me and that it was breaking his heart to see me doing this to myself. And thanks to my monster, it always worked. To think that he was trying to help me conquer my monster and accept this supposedly wonderful love right in front of me trumped every moment of truth that presented itself. My fear of walking away from true love, in error, and living alone terrorized me. This fear was my greatest weakness, and his best tool.

From then on, whenever I would call him at home from work, midweek, to my dread, I'd hear the same sexual moanings. Most times, he'd be in the bathtub when I called. When I'd ask him about it, he would insist nothing was going on, as he groaned in sexual pleasure. Was he rubbing some sick secret in my face? How could he allow me to hear this and then deny that anything was happening? Many times, I would race home, only to find him in bed, alone, seeming to anticipate my surprise appearance. I began to wonder if he somehow knew where I was when away from him. There were times he said things that he could only know if he had been with me.

Grasping at straws, I decided to put an invisible snooper program on my computer to find some proof of his lies. He was always on my computer when I was away, but rarely on it when I was there. I installed and tested it several times before deciding it worked. I'm a bit of a computer geek, so I knew what I was doing. Oddly enough, anytime I tried to see what he was up to, the program wouldn't work. In defeat, I remember losing it one night in my apartment. I fell to my hands and knees crying and screaming out in desperation, "WHO ARE YOU?" None of it made sense, and my heart was being slowly ripped apart. He couldn't be doing all of this alone. Who was this person I was so hopelessly in love with? And why wouldn't anybody tell me the truth?

About this time, one face in the crowd, Fred, started spending more time with us, working his way into our inner circle. I quickly fell into like with him, really enjoying his wacky sense of humor and the grounding nature his presence brought. I also noticed that he didn't seem to have any particular allegiance to Seth and Ray the way most everyone else did. In fact, Seth and Ray both seemed to be a little guarded toward him and his motives. I found it refreshing to have someone around who wasn't constantly off whispering with them and the others or giving me back-handed compliments and the cold shoulder. Fred treated me with respect and showed a genuine interest in my feelings and me. He seemed to know when things were getting crazy and uncomfortable for me. In those times, he'd check in with me to make sure I was okay. If I needed to go for a walk and talk, he dropped what he was doing and we'd take a walk. His counsel helped me at a time when I had nobody to help me understand what was going on. We started spending more time together, talking about everything, good and bad.

Like Matthew, he cautioned me about Seth and Ray in a general way, warning me not to let them take advantage of me, and he even suggested that I should try to slow down our partying. He knew that I paid for everything and offered ways for me to protect myself from being completely used. I remember the way he'd write down directives and talking points, sometimes with lipstick on the bathroom mirror, as we brainstormed ways to overcome the problems of the day, all while primping to go out. It felt like big sister concern and advice. I didn't let anyone know that Fred was helping me behind the scenes. He was too valuable to me to risk it.

Initially, he didn't try to get me to end things with Seth, but he coached me on how to make things better. But after being around for a while and seeing what was going on, he started persuading me to stand up for myself and consider leaving the relationship.

Most Sundays, Seth had to leave the partying in order to host open-house events. One Sunday morning, after we'd returned home from the clubs, we took a little time for lovemaking before he had to go.

"I'm going to take a shower, baby. Do you want to pour us a G shot?"

"Sure love," I replied. I happily knew what this meant. Immediately, I turned on some nice music and then pulled out our bag of chemical toys, poured a couple shots, and then went into the bedroom to pull the blankets back, lit some candles, undressed, and climbed into bed. Though he was soon going to leave me to do what he did every Sunday afternoon without me, right now we were going to make love, and this made me very happy. He didn't always make this time for us. Somehow I believed that if we made love before he left, he'd have no desire to play away from me. I told myself he was really doing what he said he was doing, even though I knew he probably wasn't. I was a fool in love.

To intensify our passion on these drug-fueled weekends, we'd often consume some GHB beforehand. One shot of G and sex became insatiable, especially after having been awake for several days on meth and ecstasy. For me, the intensity of the pleasure became the leading cause of my addiction to this new world of chemical-based pleasure. The drugs became a means to an end for me. Sex may never be as incredible as it was during that time of my life. When you walk away from that life, you have to re-learn how to enjoy life without the influence of the drugs. It's not easy to do, but worth every ounce of the struggle. You will discover that the quality of your life will improve, if you just stick with it.

My response to G was always an unknown; most times I'd handle it okay, but many times not. This time I fell out right in the middle of our passion. When I woke up several hours later, Seth was long gone. It took me a little bit to clear my head, realize where I was, and put the pieces together. When I did, I flew out of bed horrified with embarrassment, ran to the living room, snatched my cell phone from the coffee table, and dialed his number. I expected him to be really upset, but to my surprise, he wasn't.

"Seth, what happened?" It was a needless question.

"You fell out again."

"Oh God, I'm so sorry."

"It's okay," he said. His usual response to my falling out was anger. "I need to tell you something though."

"What?"

"You have to promise you won't be mad," he says.

"Why would I be mad, Seth?"

"When you were passed out, I did something kind of bad."

"What?"

"I didn't stop making love to you."

Silence.

"You what? Seth, what are you telling me?"

"David, you promised you wouldn't be mad."

"No I didn't. Did I know what was happening?"

"No," he said in a long, drawn-out breath.

"So you had sex with a dead person?"

"Oh come on, you weren't dead."

"I was in a G-hole, Seth. I could have been in a *coma*."

"But you weren't!"

"You didn't know that. You had sex with a limp piece of meat. Oh my God, Seth, that's is so wrong." Disgusted, I hung up the phone and began to cry.

He tried several times to call me back, but I didn't answer. I was in a state of shock and didn't know how to process what I had just heard.

After a long shower of intense scrubbing, I took several Tylenol PM and climbed into bed. I slept until my alarm went off on Monday morning. I didn't even know if he came home that night. I didn't care.

I called Fred from work that morning to tell him what had happened. I needed someone to know. He freaked out and went into high gear trying to get me to leave the relationship. And he nearly succeeded.

The following weekend, Seth was out of town at a retreat with his creative group. I was supposed to join him but I defied his orders and decided to stay home.

"David, why aren't you here yet?"

"Seth, I'm not coming."

"What? Are you out of your fucking mind? What is wrong with you? You said you were coming. You'd better get here, now!"

"Seth, I'm not coming. I need a break from you."

"David, don't do this. You promised that you would come here. You need to keep your word. I need you to be with me. Please come."

"I know I promised, Seth, but I can't do it. I need some time away from you. I need to clear my head, baby. I don't like what I'm feeling about us."

"No, you need to be here with me. You promised me. If you don't come here, it's over."

"Please don't threaten me, Seth."

"God damn it, David. You'd better get your ass here, now!"

With that, I hung up, threw my phone across the room, and sunk deeper into the couch. My heart breaking, I cried myself to sleep.

When I awoke, I sat in the dark for a long while, thinking about everything that was happening in my life. My conclusions didn't seem believable, yet I couldn't deny the things I was experiencing. I became angry and decided to call Fred. He said I needed to have some fun and try to forget everything for a while. I was about to medicate my broken heart with drugs and clubs, a typical form of therapy for everyone in this scene. And Fred was happy to oblige.

I was sure I'd ended the relationship that weekend, but when Seth came back, Ray jumped in with his biased form of therapy and saved us. As we sat at the dining room table, I watched helplessly as Ray wove his powerful web of manipulation. All the work Fred had done proved futile. I was confused, as insecure as ever, and still hopelessly in love with Seth. The moment he switched back into the tender caring loving boyfriend, I fell back into the trance, and everything seemed to return to that blissful perfect illusion he had created when we first began to date.

Our make-up, break-up, make-up, break-up pattern continued. In the hopes of eliminating this virus to our love, I agreed to see a couples counselor. With my distrust of Seth and the situation, I made sure it was I who chose the therapist.

Unfortunately, Seth was able to manipulate the sessions to look like I was just a jealous boyfriend and he the innocent partner. Even today my therapist admits that Seth had him duped in those early days. But he also told with me that nobody could keep a game going forever. If someone were being dishonest, that dishonestly would eventually be revealed.

Somehow in the middle of all this, Seth and I decided to move in together. When the pendulum swung to the other extreme, providing blinding moments of joy and happiness, such a move felt like a natural progression. High on the bliss of the fleeting moment, we toured my building with the strangely aware property manager. The way she studied us, it was obvious to me that she knew more than she dared to speak. Like newlyweds, we danced from unit to unit, pondering floor plans and closet space. Finally we settled on a two-bedroom corner unit one floor down from where I currently lived. It even had a small view of the Space Needle. This move was going to solve all of our problems. We were sure of it. Whenever we were happy and drama-free, the love I felt for him quickly erased all the pain we had been through. I believed in our love. I knew we were going to make it.

Not long after our happy house search, the arguing resumed though, quickly convincing me this was the wrong thing to do. But Seth became determined that this move would happen and wouldn't accept anything but yes. When I tried to get him to see that it was a bad idea, he imposed an ultimatum of us getting the place together or breaking up forever. Backed into a corner, I turned to my therapist for guidance. I went into that session thinking he would help me convince Seth that we should wait until things were more stable. But Seth had successfully woven his web. When Michael endorsed it, failing to see any problem, I became silently enraged. I couldn't believe what was happening. I just sat there in shock, staring at Seth with an anger that was surely palpable. I trusted my growing intuition about him, but I couldn't understand how our therapist could be fooled by his obvious manipulation.

Feeling hopelessly defeated, I stopped therapy and reluctantly signed the new lease with Seth. I can still remember that day as we sat in the manager's office. I was filled with so much silent rage as I signed the paperwork. On a deep level, I knew I was making a mistake, but I felt powerless to stop it. I still loved him and I was powerless because of it. I was so afraid to make a mistake that I couldn't fix with an apology. I didn't want to miss my one chance at everlasting love. But I knew something wasn't right about him. And I was now locked into a year of living in this desperate situation. What the hell was I thinking?

Moving day and Valentine's Day arrived as one. Two reasons to feel ecstatic about life, and they were lost on me. Feeling alone and worn down by everything, I was doing my best to cope under the dull throb of my mental and emotional wounds. I couldn't make sense of anything in my life, and I didn't have the energy to care. I was living life through a deep depression now.

It wasn't until I was nearly home from work that I remembered what day it was. *God, if I arrive home without the expected tokens of love, he'll certainly crush any remaining desire I have to continue breathing.* Even though I loved him, my heart was battered and I didn't feel like celebrating this lover's holiday. I think I understood in that pain what a dog might feel for his master who simultaneously kicks and cuddles him.

Through it all, my love for him remained. It seems easy to look back at the situation and wonder how anyone could struggle to know what to do when things should have been so obvious. But I don't think anyone could ever expect that his entire life would be overtaken by deception, especially if that life was as ordinary as mine. Kings and queens had to worry about lies and deception this grand, not common middle-class Americans like me.

When I arrived home, Ray was in my current apartment, packing my things. I felt violated to have him going through all my belongings, but I made no issue of it because I didn't have the strength to defend myself from the nastiness that came so easy to him. Sensing my building irritation or just wanting me to go away, he quickly directed me to Seth, who was waiting for me in the new place downstairs. *Great, what are they up to now?*

I just wanted to climb into bed, pull the covers over my head, and sleep until it all went away. Instead, I somberly made my way down to the new place. When I walked in, I heard Seth in the kitchen and some soft music playing in the background. In the way a smell can transport you to another place and time, the music did this. I instantly imagined things were different, our painful history erased. In this fantasy, I was a joyously happy man and Seth loved me without fault. The warmth of our home penetrated my blood as I walked through the door, followed by his smiling face, glowing in the love he felt for me. It seemed so real; I could even smell the dinner he had prepared. My head began to spin, surely caused by my needing it to be real. As I turned the corner, I realized the aroma in my nose wasn't coming from the fantasy world my mind had journeyed to. Though the apartment was still empty, he had prepared a Valentine's dinner for us, complete with an indoor picnic arranged upon a sheet on the dining room floor. The fantasy in my mind and this reality instantly melded into one.

I slipped into a foggy daze, experiencing everything in slow, surreal motions. Like glamour shot portraits, everything was softened and perfect. I handed him the flowers and we hugged really hard for what felt a perfectly eternal moment. In that moment I had my baby back and nothing else in the universe mattered.

He sat me down at our romantic table on the floor, poured some wine, and served dinner. The perfume of the roses he had arranged seemed to dance in the flickering glow of the candles. He served his delicious sesame chicken and cauliflower in a cheddar cheese sauce. *Oh God, this is the medicine my soul needed.* As I took that first bite, looking at him through the candlelight, tears began to roll down my face, the salty brine combining with the food in my mouth. As wonderful as this moment felt, as perfectly as he had fulfilled my longing to again experience the perfection of our beginning, somewhere in me I knew this was just an illusion that would quickly fade away. Those tears dripping onto my plate represented my grief in knowing this beautiful moment wouldn't last beyond the night and my weariness as to what was sure to follow.

Our Happy Home

As expected, the sketch and drama with Seth returned almost overnight. Something about moving into the new place brought with it a new level of strangeness. It also provided the first solid bits of evidence of his secrets. I began to assemble enough pieces of the puzzle to reveal glimpses of the hidden story. Yet, I was so hopelessly entangled in the web that I wouldn't be able to escape until I was left with no choice but to live or die.

Ray's role as Seth's right-hand man continued to develop and he now became closely involved in our lives. Initially I was suspect of his relatively swift change of attitude toward me, but I also found some easing comfort in it, and in that comfort, I failed to recognize what he was doing. In reality, he became our own perverse version of Dr. Phil, helping us to work through the ever-present arguing, though he'd shamelessly side with Seth every time and carefully twist my thoughts in the process. Some well scripted hugs and clever distractions at the end ensured I would let go of my conclusions and accept his diagnosis.

The frustration I felt each time he finished analyzing me—and us—had me crawling up the walls in a silent scream. I couldn't understand why they screwed with my head the way they did. Each time, my only choice seemed to be to concede if I hoped to escape the skull session. I understood, even more than I realized at the time, the cause of any given argument, but because so much of the story was still obscure to me then, I could never get to the source, to enough of the truth to put the pieces together. After Ray finished scrambling my brain, I might as well have had my head up my ass because nothing made any sense.

Getting my belongings down to the new place was easy enough with their help, but we also had to move Seth from his apartment, which was several blocks away. We borrowed a truck from a friend and moved his big furniture in a couple of loads, planning to move the smaller stuff later, in our cars. After stacking everything in the garage close to the elevator, and before moving everything up to the apartment, Seth and I left to return the truck. We were gone 30 minutes at the most. When we returned, everything had been moved into our apartment, and Ray was sitting on the couch waiting for us. He sat there with a glorious look of pride, begging me to ask how he had done it. Flabbergasted, I did, asking who had helped him move everything so quickly. It was physically impossible to move such big furniture by himself, and in such a short amount of time. But he claimed he had accomplished the feat all by himself. Clearly he had help, but why he wouldn't reveal who it was or why he felt the need to conceal it, I didn't know.

As we settled in and unpacked the boxes, I immediately noticed the noise of tinkering within the walls, the sound of wires moving within the drywall. This carried on for several weeks. Oddly enough, it didn't initially occur to me that this could be anything sinister. It was a brand-new building, and some construction around the premises hadn't been completed when I was moving in. In a curious synchronicity, Seth pointed out an outlet in the kitchen that had black char around it, a plug that had been healthy on previous inspection. He and Ray made a bit of a spectacle of it, notably *wondering what in the world* could be the cause. Growing accustomed to their flair for unknowable drama, I flippantly and sarcastically said I'd have the management look into it. Seth then jumped in and said, "Nothing to worry about, babe. I'll handle it."

That weekend, when we planned to move the rest of his stuff, more twilight zone drama occurred. Friday had arrived, so getting high did too. And guess what? We argued. When that happened, I attempted to prevent the conclusion of the move, hoping to provide an 11th-hour escape. No luck. Instead, I was enlisted to help him pack up what was left in his place and move it to ours, all during the wee hours of the weekend. About 3 am, while we were at his place packing, flying on Chris and Ellen (*who moves on Ecstasy and Meth?*), the atmosphere was cold and strained. Out of the blue, Peter and a couple of unknown associates arrived at Seth's door, bathed in a mischievous aura of high. Peter was a shady criminal whom Seth had introduced to the group before my arrival. When I asked him about it, Seth swore he didn't know of Peter's criminal background. (Peter became roommates with Ray not long after. Turns out, he's a person with another name, another life, and a lengthy criminal history, which wasn't all history, as marshals from somewhere back east arrived at Ray's door with guns in hand, looking for him. Peter was also well connected to a ring of burglars; this "caught everyone by surprise.")

The apartment complex Seth was moving from was supposedly secure, requiring the occupant to buzz visitors past two separate entrances to gain access to his front door. We never heard a buzz; just suddenly Peter was at the door.

"Hey Seth, what's going on?" Peter says. He and two others are standing in the front door. We had propped the door open to move boxes out into the hall near the elevator. Seth looks at me and then back at them. It's obvious they are just as high as we are.

"Hi Peter." Seth drops the screwdriver he is using to disassemble the computer desk and walks closer to them. Seth pretends surprise, but it's obvious that the meeting has been planned, for they don't play along.

"Give me a couple minutes. We're close to leaving," Seth says. He steps out in the hall for a quick exchange with the three. I strain to listen but hear nothing. He comes back in, pulls a trash bag from under the sink, opens the fridge and packs up the dozen or so bags of coffee from his freezer. "Let's take this load."

Knowing that something strange is happening, I agree and follow him out the door. The others are gone. We load the elevator, the doors close, and we begin to descend to the garage. When the doors open, he tries to get away.

"I'll take this to the trash and meet you at the car," he says.

"I've got it." I snatch the bag from his hands. I know this bag of coffee holds the answer to what is happening.

"David, don't." He seems worried.

I turn and head into the trash room. As soon as the bag leaves my fingers, crashing down 10 feet into the dumpster, I notice the doors open on the black Suburban parked in the alley. Three guys climb out and head toward the other entrance to the trash room. Seth quickly pulls me from the room and slams the door behind us. I sense the worry in his eyes and decide to say nothing.

After we load the last items into his car, Seth insists I return home, that he needs to get gas. I can see the Suburban sitting in the alley, parking lights on, the engine running. They are waiting. I try to talk him into allowing me to follow him to the gas station, even offering to pay for the gas, but he refuses, saying he'll be right behind me. I know he is lying, but I give in. I see something in his eyes that makes me afraid. I get into my car, and as I'm driving away, I look in my rear view mirror and see him follow the Suburban in the other direction.

Once home, I repeatedly phone him, but no luck. I fall into an emotional blackout filled with fear, rage, and panic. I don't know what is happening and I'm terrified.

When he finally arrives home, he is messy and much higher than when I had left him. Disgusted, I go directly to the medicine cabinet, take several Tylenol PM, and climb into bed alone.

Time passes. By now, whatever normalcy I remember of my life prior to Seth is fading away, being replaced by the growing darkness of the netherworld that is taking over. Each week brings with it more and more mystery and pain. Seth does his best to inject normal activity into the mix to keep my heart entranced and my mind confused. Weeknights, when I arrive home from work, he awakes from his daily slumber and we eat dinner together on the couch in front of the TV, snuggle, and fall asleep. Monday through Thursday continues to be drug-free. The illusion of a happy home he is providing is the perfect distraction to evaporate the craziness of the weekends. We engage in little to no socializing during the week. Because the weekends happen under the influence of drugs, by contrast the week-days appear relatively normal. I find myself midweek wondering if it is all a dream. Midweek, a casual observer might even think there is nothing about our household that is different from that of any other typical gay couple. But as time goes on, even that begins to lose out to the growing strangeness that is becoming my life.

During my hours at work, the agonizing phone conversations filled with his sexual moanings became more commonplace. My curiosity about the source of what I was hearing drove me into a continually deeper and more obsessive search for answers. I knew that what I was witnessing wasn't just the simple answer that he was being unfaithful to me. Because of everything I was learning about Seth and his world, I understood that my simple ideas about sex couldn't explain what I was hearing. And I knew that this bizarre sexual activity was going to shepherd me to the answers I was searching for. Every discovery I made, every clue I uncov-ered led me closer and closer to some clandestine sexual truth that they were going to incredible effort to keep secret.

The baffling part to me was how Seth believed he could let me, or any inti-mate partner into his life, and not expect him to discover his secrets. Why did he let me in? Did he think he could manage to pull it off and have his cake and frost-ing too? Or did he expect my reaction? I began to wonder if he wanted me to notice what nobody but an intimate partner could notice about his life. It takes that kind of intimacy to reveal what I was discovering about him. I wonder if it was all part of his plan.

Initially I thought the weird moaning and sexual behavior was the result of some kind of personal vibrating device, though it seemed absurd that anything so ridiculously common would drive Seth and his friends to such great attempts to conceal the truth. Studying everyone's actions and especially Seth's, I became convinced that I should pursue this angle.

About this time the gang had started a curious new behavior when we were out at the clubs, a behavior that seemed to be pushing me to delve deeper into the mystery. One night at Contour, while we were on the dance floor, I noticed that many had attached a small stuffed animal onto the waistband of their pants, just off to the right of the crotch area. It was a little pink elephant. Other times, they had it stuffed down their pants, always off to the right, with just the head poking out. Whenever I'd ask what it meant, they'd just flash a mischievous smile and turn away. When I asked Seth, he'd say, "I don't know. Why don't you ask them?" knowing full well I'd already attempted to. Playing off each other, they'd seem to be finding some hidden pleasure in the silliness of it all. I quit asking and just added it to my mental list of reasons why I should continue my search. It also added to the defiant anger that was building inside me.

I scoured the Internet looking for some small vibrating device that one could wear out in public. Hours and hours of looking, but nothing I ran across fit the bill.

During my search, I also started looking for evidence that I was being secretly videotaped. Web cams were becoming popular in chat rooms, with people throwing sex parties for any invited guest to watch. In the sketchiness of all that was going on around me, things were said that made me feel like I was being watched. The way Seth and others would look off into odd directions while in our apartment, as though performing for a camera, made me wonder what they were looking at. Seth had been doing this since I met him, back in his apartment, and now it was happening in our new place. He made reference to things I did that he could only know if he were watching me when I was alone. He did this especially when we were having sex. His friends implied more of the same when they were visiting.

When I started to inquire about it and wonder aloud if such a thing could be going on, with dramatic flair, Seth tried to shut down my thinking. He went out of his way to embarrass me with it and tell me how stupid I was behaving. One night as we were all heading out to the clubs, he had just finished sharing his joke of my fears with everyone at our pre-funk when I overheard Heyden whispering to someone, "He's going to be pissed when he finds out what's really going on."

One particular Sunday afternoon, Seth had left to go to his weekly open house commitment, leaving me to my usual home alone routine. I had become unsure of what he was really doing because most times when I called him there, I'd discover him writhing in orgasmic behavior, just like I would when calling him from work. Surely he couldn't be working in that condition. Of course, we were both sketchy and high, having come to the finale of another weekend of intense partying. I spent the time on my endless Internet search for answers to the mystery. For some reason, on this particular day, the noises within the walls and coming from the unit above ours caught my attention in a way it hadn't before. It occurred to me that maybe this had something to do with my feelings of being watched. I decided to investigate.

I began moving around my apartment, going from room to room and listening intently. I pretended to be doing things, going to the bathroom, straightening up, anything so as not to bring attention to what I was really doing. I began to notice very light whispering, so faint it almost wasn't there. I initially attributed this to that fact that I was high. But then I realized that the noises above and around me were following me from room to room. I began studying each room, looking for anywhere a camera could be hidden; eventually I gave up trying to conceal my efforts. While standing on the toilet, pulling at the vent in the ceiling, I heard some noises in the space above me. In faint whispering, I heard a voice ask, "What's he doing?" My reaction was instantaneous.

Nearly falling off the toilet, I stumbled backward into the wall, and in horror yelled, "Oh my God, oh my God! They *are* watching me! It's real! Oh shit! People are watching me!" I paced from room to room, talking aloud like this.

Part of my response was genuine, and part of it was for show. If there were people watching me, I wanted them to know I knew.

Finally I said aloud, "I have to call the police. I'm going to call the police." (Think of Sally Fields in *Mrs. Doubtfire*, the moment when she realizes that her husband is disguised as the nanny.) I then searched for my cell phone and opened it to dial. What happened next blew my mind.

All of a sudden I heard wires all over the apartment being ripped from the walls and a storm of commotion exploded all around me. People were running around above and doors were slamming. I ran out to the hallway and heard people stumbling through the stairwells and the elevator doors were opening and closing, the bell ringing over and over. I quickly ran back into the apartment and locked the door. I grabbed my phone, intending to call the police, but every time I started to dial, I stopped in fear. So much was happening. I was fearful that calling the police wasn't such a good idea. I went out on the balcony to see if I could look up into the window of the unit above. Instead, below, I saw people running out of the lobby and onto the sidewalk with boxes of video equipment and rolls of cable in their arms. They were frantically talking and pointing each other in different directions. Most jumped into the cars, vans, and trucks parked on the street directly in front of the building; the rest fled in every direction, trying to make their escape. Engines roared to life, and the sound of peeling rubber filled the air as they raced away. I fell into an uncontrollable fit of trembling anxiety. My heart was beating so hard it felt like I was having a heart attack.

I ran through my apartment, holding my phone, but I couldn't convince myself to dial the police. In my drug-induced paranoia, the longer I thought about my situation, the more afraid I became. I knew I had to do something, but what?

The only person I knew to call was Jeff, but he was in California visiting his mom that weekend. I didn't want to call him in my condition. We had remained close, and he had some idea of my fears about Seth, but I had never felt so afraid that I needed to pull him into the immediate drama. In that moment I realized I had absolutely nobody but him to help me. Because of my insecurities, and Seth's controlling nature, other than Jeff, I'd allowed my world to dwindle to just Seth and his people.

"Hi Jeff. Can you talk?"

"Sure. Are you okay? What's wrong?"

"I'm in trouble. I need some help. Something really weird just happened, and I'm not sure what to do."

"What's wrong?"

"Remember the videotaping I told you about? Well, I just got confirmation that it is really happening. I heard them, Jeff, and when I said I was going to call the police, all hell broke loose. I could hear wires being ripped from the walls, and people were running everywhere to get away. They had video equipment. There were so many of them, running out the front door, getting into cars. I don't know what to do, Jeff. I am really scared."

"Calm down, honey. It will be okay. What's happening now? Where's Seth"

"He's not here. They all left. Jeff, it's real. I told you it was, all of it. I don't know what to do. What if they come back?"

"They won't, you scared them away. But you need to get the hell out of there. Do you still have my key?"

"Yes."

"Then go to my house. Just get out of there. Do you hear me? You need to get out of there."

"Okay, okay. Stay by your phone. Jeff, I wish you were here, I need you."

"It'll be okay, I promise. But you need to get out of there."

"I love you."

"I love you too. Call me when you get to my place."

After I hung up, I planned to go to his apartment, but that never happened. The paranoia that increased over the next hour overwhelmed my mind with perilous events that might arise if I were to leave my apartment. I knew I couldn't risk driving, and the four-block walk to his place might as well have been a midnight journey through the forests of Transylvania considering my state of mind.

A few hours later, the drugs began to wear off and my head had had some time to clear from the adrenaline. I managed to calm myself down and did some heavy thinking about the quagmire my situation presented. I knew Seth would be home in a few hours, and I hadn't yet settled on what to do next.

It's interesting to me how my mental processes were dealing with all of these bizarre events. Even just a few hours after this undeniable incident, I noticed myself considering that maybe I had overreacted, that maybe it wasn't what I thought. Maybe that was because this was the pattern I had become used to. This "expose, remove, and deny" had become central to Seth and Ray's M.O. They would show me very strange things about their lives, then remove me from the situation, and ultimately deny anything strange had ever happened. During these weekends, they took me down into their rabbit hole, followed by a carefully orchestrated process of disinformation. The past few hours felt the same.

Initially, I wondered why anyone would go to so much effort to videotape me. While replaying all the events in my mind since meeting Seth, I quickly realized what it must be about. Sex. Seth's entire world centered on it. My world too had morphed into one of sex after meeting him. We met in a sexual chat room. The central focus of everything we did and everyone we knew revolved around sex and drugs. Even this mysterious secret I was discovering swirled around sex. So why me? Why would someone so unconnected and unknowing be a direct target? Just asking that question provided me with an immediate answer, though a horrifying one.

All this time, I had been struggling to understand why Seth didn't seem to have much interest in satisfying my sexual needs and desires. Initially he did, but it faded quickly. Soon, our sex became all about my satisfying his needs. In time, it was only I who took care of my needs. It took me a while to accept that this was happening. I looked after his needs nearly every day, something he raved about. For me, it was pure pleasure. I was happy to do this for my partner. I enjoyed it. He didn't reciprocate much though, always telling me he felt bad about it, but always having a reason not to take that little step for his lover. We messed around often enough, but rarely did he take the time to genuinely pleasure me. Without the drugs and the emphasis that he placed on sex, it might not have bothered me so much. But the combination of the two had an overpowering effect on me. The drugs and sexual intoxication were nearly impossible to ignore. By the time Sunday rolled around, the only thing on anybody's mind in this world was sex.

Each Sunday, around noon, when the club started to wind down, everyone would race off with whoever was hosting a group event to finish off the partying marathon with sex. Seth kept me away from any of that. And every Sunday afternoon, Seth had to head off to his open house, leaving me at home, high and horny. We had agreed to monogamy, so masturbation became my private friend.

Most Sunday afternoons, there I'd be, whacking away for the hours while he was gone. Very creative, uninhibited Ecstasy- and GHB-fueled self-pleasuring. And surely, I realized, this is what the videotaping was all about.

I concluded it was best to do nothing. Considering the fact that I was high and freaked out about what I had just witnessed, and knowing Seth's reaction would be fierce and unforgiving, I knew that any rash move would prove disastrous. I straightened things up and tried to make it seem like nothing out of the ordinary had taken place while he was gone.

When Seth returned, I could tell by the way he was looking at me that he knew everything. Calculating and silent, he looked around suspiciously. Then he looked at me with a burning anger, like a provoked wild animal. In this moment, I realized I had seen this performance before.

"How was your afternoon?" he asked.

"It was okay, I guess. I just listened to music and straightened up a bit. How was yours?"

"It was fine," he said coldly. His eyes searched the apartment. I watched him move from room to room, pausing and looking suspiciously at the places where I had engaged in drug-fueled masturbation. He also seemed to register the places where I had noticed voices and wires being pulled out.

I pretended not to notice, and in doing that, I guess this time it was me who directed this sketchy weekend back to illusion. Something had changed though, something he seemed to realize too. We both learned something on this day. Because of this weekend, my eyes were open. I knew something very strange was going on in my life and I felt emboldened to search for proof of it. The deception that felt like common knowledge to everyone but me became impossible to deny. And I became less fearful of anyone knowing I was searching for that truth. I suddenly knew without a doubt that I wasn't experiencing just paranoid fear, but something very real and strange.

One Sunday morning not long after, a weekend I insisted we stay home and sober, we decided to go out for breakfast. We walked a few blocks to Glo's Diner, a popular little dive famous for breakfast. It was busy as usual, so we had to wait for a table. I went inside to leave my name with the host, while Seth remained outside. Standing at the counter in the crook of the little V-shaped cafe waiting for service, I noticed a cook, a very attractive young man, looking at me intently, like he recognized me from somewhere. He must have figured it out because he got very excited and started laughing at some private joke. He then grabbed the attention of another boy working with him and pointed at me. He mimed exaggerated masturbation and then pointed back at me. The other boy looked at me. He too seemed to recognize me and they went on laughing together.

I had a pretty good idea what it was all about, and I ran out the door enraged and humiliated. I started yelling at Seth, telling him what happened. I blamed him, knowing that nothing of this had existed until he came into my life. He immediately turned to his usual rhetoric, that I was just imagining things. We argued as we walked away, and I grabbed him by the shoulders, pulled his face to mine, and pouring all my fear and rage into his eyes, assured him that if he were in any way connected to this I would kill him. And I meant it. And he knew it.

Life for me was deteriorating noticeably now, both physically and mentally. The arguing with Seth gradually grew in intensity and inevitably crossed over into the physical. It started with him slapping me across the face whenever I showed signs that I was falling out on my GHB doses. He defended the move, explaining that he was attempting to pull me out of my fall. I remember the surprised faces of those witnessing his brutal compassion. This abuse usually happened in full view of those in the club. Because I was falling out, I could do little more than share a moment of startled bewilderment before slipping back into my uncontrollable teetering on the brink of unconsciousness.

Once, while we were arguing in our bedroom, my back turned to him, he lurched out and kicked me on my ass, knocking me down into the dresser. In his final attacks before I frightened him into keeping his hands off of me, whenever his temper would boil over, he'd wrap his hands around my neck. This moment of desperation happened four times, and each time my reaction to escape was intense and swift. Physical abuse pushed me too far. After those four episodes, I put a forceful, threatening end to it. Though I was much stronger than he and I very much wanted to return the gesture, I never found the permission within myself to hit back. The verbal rage I poured onto him while I ripped his hands from my neck thankfully brought his physical impulses to an end. There burned a deep red fire within me during those moments with his hands around my neck, a fire he surely saw.

My defiance was intensifying, probably in relation to Seth's temper and physical behavior, not to mention the craziness of the periphery. My growing frustration and the toll it was having on my mind expressed itself as a deep, brewing anger, an anger that also, fortunately for me, stood guard, protecting me at my most fearful and perilous moments. I was losing control of everything and still couldn't understand how and why all of this was happening to me.

Seth continually insisted he had nothing to do with it, a baseless claim that only added to my confused and ravaged heart. Love sure made me stupid in those days.

Out at the clubs, the energy around me was shifting too. Before, I had always been welcomed into the crowd as warmly as Seth, Ray, or any of the others. But now, hardly anyone would talk to me, and if they did, the insincerity of their interest was plainly visible. I struggled through many futile attempts to mingle my way through those terrifying nights, surrounded by the ever-present groups of baneful, hostile eyes watching my every movement while they carried on in their hushed, private whisperings. When I'd pass in earshot, the talk would most always stop, replaced by uninviting forced smiles, but once in a while I'd overhear bits of conversation, including "that bitch is going crazy" or "she's turning him into a G-whore," and "what a mess," all undoubtedly meant for me to hear as I drifted by. Not much in that world happened by accident or without purpose. But despite their rejection, I was now part of their world. I knew too much for them to eject me with a simple cold shoulder. I knew their scene, their drugs, their sex, and their secrets. They had used all of this to hurt me. I knew this, and I now needed to know everything about them to understand why. I had to know why.

Driving north on Interstate 5 on my way home from work, a car pulls up on the left side of me and holds there. I look over to see two 20-something boys in the front seats, both looking at me and smiling. They're giggling. The passenger holds up a bumper sticker that says I LOVE GAY PORN. They laugh and stare at me before speeding away. When I get home, still shaking and fuming in my anger, I tell Seth what has happened.

"I'm sick of this shit, Seth. I'm going to hire a private detective. I will find out what is going on, and you better hope you are not part of it."

"Oh, come on, David. Please tell me you're not serious. I'm sure it had nothing to do with you."

"I'm dead serious, Seth. Of course it did. That shit doesn't just happen."

And I really was going to hire a private detective to get to the bottom of things. But after my passion storm faded, I realized it would be pointless. Seth seemed impossibly ahead of me in a way that I began to think I would never escape. Whatever was going on, I knew it was larger than anything I could hope to uncover with my meager resources.

I guess I mostly said it to see his reaction. He remained calm and cool as usual, but he looked worried this time. Later that night, when he was asleep on the couch, I noticed he had left the browser on his computer running, still logged into his web mail. Maybe it was a ruse, but I don't think so. He was tired that day, and I realized this was a rare chance to do some investigating, so I snooped. An email exchange between him and Ray was still available. In it, he told Ray about the incident and my intentions to delve deeper. Ray replied "Shut the fuck up!" Seth then replied, "I don't care, they'll know it wasn't me."

Someone Take This Pain Away

It's a strange thing when you arrive at your breaking point. How the most ordinary and benign event can push you over the edge. The proverbial straw that broke the camel's back. This moment had arrived for me.

It was a day like any other. I arrived home from work to find Seth asleep as he was nearly every weekday afternoon. We weren't on good terms this day, so the heaviness of this weighed on my heart.

I drop my workbag in its usual spot and start flipping through the mail. Not expecting anything unusual, I open a letter from my auto insurance company, informing me that because of the two claims I had processed with them during the previous year, they are raising my monthly premium from $150 to $480.

OH MY GOD! I am filled with fear and despair. Surely this has to be a mistake. I immediately call the customer service number intending to clear this up.

The voice on the other end is cold. In typical "I-don't-give-a-shit-about-you" corporate fashion, she assures me this is no mistake.

"But I've been giving you my money for over a decade. Now you tell me that my insurance bill is more than my car payment? I can't afford this; I will have to sell my car. How can you people do this? It's not right."

"I'm sorry, sir, there is nothing I can do for you."

Enraged, I throw my phone across the room. "Goddamn it!"

I was crushed. Money worries had already started making a home alongside the growing fear in my mind. Having spent nearly all my savings supporting Seth and me, my funds were running low. His agreement to pay just a third of the rent rarely happened nor did he help with anything else. I was the sugar daddy.

Later that afternoon, Jeff calls, wanting to invite me out for a drink. We don't spend much time together anymore, so it feels good to receive his call. At first I say no, but it doesn't take too much arm-twisting to convince me to join him. Considering the day, I figure I can use a distraction. I know he is an honest, caring friend I can count on for emotional support.

Seth tries to keep me from going. Always threatened by my relationship with Jeff, he leaps at any opportunity to pull me away from him. On this day, I am in no mood to argue with him. I give him a look that says, "Don't even try," and walk out the door.

We meet up at RPlace, a neighborhood pub just up the street. This is our favorite place to have a beer together, though the usual uplifting nature of our visits doesn't come to pass on this night. He tries everything to cheer me up, but after a couple of drinks, I grow more depressed, so I cut it short and head home. The moment I walk away from him, I start falling apart. When I arrive home, Seth isn't there. He has left to attend his improv rehearsal.

I pour myself a glass of wine and sit at my computer. I launch iTunes and select the MusicOne station. I launch my budget program and study my finances. It's hopeless. All the while, my mind drifts under the spell Seth has cast over me, trying to make sense of what I've become.

As I sit there in hopeless misery, I begin noticing the lyrics of a song that is playing. The beat is wonderful and deep, but the lyrics are what really stand out at me. "Yet Another Day" by Armin van Buuren tells the story of a man so beaten down by the mysterious life he finds himself a part of that he feels helpless to escape. It is his declaration of defeat and final goodbye. It is a suicide note set to music. Through complete surrender, I realize that it is my message to this world I no longer understand nor desire to be apart of. Like a divine message from the universe, I suddenly understand how it is going to end. I know how I will escape the invisible grip that has my life held hostage.

With a sudden calm, I download the song to my hard drive, set it to repeat, and turn the volume very loud. I print out the lyrics and study them. It is exactly what I feel. I know what to do.

I go to the party bag and retrieve the remaining doses of GHB. After pouring the noxious fluid down my throat, I pull the sleeping pills from the medicine cabinet, grab the bottle of wine from the refrigerator, switch off the lights, and settle onto the couch. I begin swallowing the pills, one at a time, with gulps of wine. The tears start to flow down my face, the wails of my last cry getting more hysterical with each pill I swallow. I am mortified at what I am doing, but I feel helpless to stop.

There is a place that exists for those who have begun the final process of dying, a place only those who are in the last moments of their life can journey to. It's not here really, but it's not there either. Maybe it's the same experience somebody who has jumped from a building has on the way down, only slower and without the dread of the violent crush at the end. Maybe it's just the knowing that it is done. I know what that place looks and feels like. I've been there.

Uncharacteristically, Seth comes home early from rehearsal. He explodes through the door with a bouquet of flowers in his hand, pretending to walk into a reality he knows isn't there. Instead, he finds me drifting into unconsciousness, my death song pouring through the air. He runs up to me, slaps me across the face, and cries out in feigned horror, even though I am sure he knew what he was walking into before he burst through that door. I know it's all an act. I know we aren't alone.

The next events are blurry. Medics arrive, people begin cutting my clothes from me, and others attach medical equipment to my body and ask me too many irritating questions. Lights flash in my eyes. Unknown faces stare into mine. In my mind I scream, "Leave me alone! Let me go! I don't want you to stop this!" On the outside, my silent body falls in and out of consciousness. Red bursts of light flash through my mind, riddled with faces of souls I've never met. Distorted bass music blasts through my head and Seth carries on in the distance. I feel myself drifting up and then I slam back down again.

Strapped to a board, I am wheeled out into the hallway, all the neighbors looking on in unabashed curiosity. Down the elevator, out the lobby door, and into the ambulance I go. The medics ask Seth if he wants to ride with us, but he says no, he'll come later. I then let go and fall out.

When I awake, I am in the emergency room. Blue people are milling about everywhere. The noise and bright lights hurt my senses. *God, I'm so cold.* There are more questions, so many questions. Seth finally arrives just before they begin shoving the tube down my throat.

"This is going to feel uncomfortable, David," the nurse says.

Oh God, it feels like they are trying to drown me! I can't breathe. Somebody help me! Please somebody help me! Again and again they try to kill me. I keep gagging and flailing, but they keep mercilessly forcing this thing down my throat. They seem angry that I won't let them kill me. They strap me to the bed and I scream in terror, hoping somebody will come to my rescue. I see Ray walk into the room; when he sees me, tears fill his eyes and he turns away. After finally getting the tube down my throat, I calm down and they pump my stomach for what feels an eternity. Finally, the terror stops, and they remove the tube.

Next, I am wheeled out into the hallway, all the way down to the dark dead end and left there alone. I drift in and out of consciousness until Seth once again joins me. Though physically exhausted, I become wide awake in his presence. It is then that I notice how high he is. *You son of a bitch! I hate you!*

He is also revealing something to me that I had previously known only by sound. For whatever reason, he feels this is the right moment to pull the curtain back on his dark secret. I guess he doesn't think I'll survive the night. With this, I begin to wonder if I will myself.

I know his reasoning for doing so must have been my drastic move and weak condition. It was only when I had put myself into such a compromised condition that he allowed such strange things to occur so openly. The visiting nurse kept taking blood, carefully noting that they were testing my liver function. Because of the deluge of acetaminophen my body had absorbed from the Tylenol PM, there was an impending fear that transplant would become necessary. My liver enzymes were spiking with no let-up. I assumed Seth believed this wasn't going to end well for me.

He is so high. I know it and so do the nurses tending to me. I can see it in their eyes when they interact with him. They don't seem to like him much. He is also under the spell of something I don't recognize.

For no good reason, he keeps pulling out his Palm Pilot and pecking away at it with the digipen. His doesn't have email or Internet capability, so it could only be for Bluetooth, or a similar technology. I know that Bluetooth allows a wireless interaction between digital signals, including nano-technologies. A use of nano-technology that isn't supposed to be in the hands of the general public yet. Until this moment, he hadn't used his Palm Pilot much, other than taking it with him on his Sunday open house gigs. He certainly hadn't used it in my presence before, so why now? Why did he need to peck away at this stupid device, at 3 in the morning, while I was in the hospital recovering from a suicide attempt that he had played a huge role in provoking?

Suddenly, something about the Palm Pilot causes him to kick into fits of passion. He looks like he is being molested by some invisible force, his crotch gyrating back and forth and his face contorting in uncontrollable pleasure. Periodically, he has to step out of my eyesight, behind my bed, for a private moment of orgasm, though he doesn't escape soon enough to escape my witness. With a sudden flood of memories, I understand why on several occasions in bathrooms at the clubs he proudly revealed to me the odd reaction he supposedly had to the drugs. I think about that heavily guarded electronic box at Contour and an event at the club. I know these events are related.

"Seth, are you okay?" I ask. I had bumped into him, knocking his sunglasses from his face. It is very dark on the dance floor, but I can see his eyes rolling around strangely in the disco lights. He looks like he is about to pass out.

"I'm fine," he says angrily. "Let's go to the bathroom." He turns and walks away.

I'm disturbed by what I'm seeing, but I follow. In the bathroom, we both stand at the urinal to pee. I keep glancing over at him, trying to figure out what is going on with him. He is acting bizarre.

"Want to see something strange?" he asks.

"What, Seth?" I'm obviously frustrated. He then reveals to me that instead of pee, semen is flowing from his penis.

"Isn't that strange?" he asks.

"What the hell? Why are you cumming?"

"This happens to me a lot when I'm partying," he replies. He then looks up from his penis and back at me, revealing a devilish smile. Suddenly, his eyes start rolling again, just as they had on the dance floor. I struggle to understand what he is doing and wonder why he feels the need to hurt me with it. Angry, I quickly leave the bathroom and escape back to the dance floor. I look back a moment later to realize he hasn't followed me. Confused, heartbroken, and sketchy, I continue to dance, hiding my terror in the music and darkness.

As I lay there in the hospital bed, again watching him in his secret pleasure, I realize he is once again begging me to address it, longing for me to open Pandora's box. If I do, I know he'll use it as an opportunity to make me look crazy and put wheels into motion that I won't be able to stop. I tried to kill myself after all. Instead, I force myself into a self-imposed act of phoniness, pretending not to understand what he is doing. He knows full well what I'm doing, and he does everything he can to thwart my escape.

"Why are you looking at me like that? What are you thinking about, David? Is something wrong? Is there something you want to ask me? It's okay. You can tell me."

If I dare to speak one word about his secret, he will pounce on me like a rabid pit bull. For reasons unknown to me, he is using his secret to manipulate me, to hurt me, and it is working perfectly, even though I try to hide this truth from him. It takes every ounce of courage in me to keep my mouth shut during these endless hours of confinement.

Suddenly I realize that nobody I trust knows where I am or what has happened to me. Instantly horrified by this, I demand he call Jeff. He refuses, insisting that if I truly love him, I would only want him taking care of me.

"You'd better get Jeff here now!" Probably sensing my growing fear and anger, he gives in and starts making the motions to fulfill my demands. He calls Heyden, his trusty friend and supplier of drugs, who lives in Jeff's building. Heyden notifies Jeff, who immediately rushes to my side. Just before he arrives, Seth, unable to mask his increasing high, insists he needs to leave.

As Jeff approaches me, walking down that long hall to my bed relegated to the back corner, I see the look of dread wash over his face. He is heartbroken when he sees my condition, noticing that I have been strapped to the bed for my own safety.

As he had a propensity to do when things spiraled out of his control, his Rock of Gibraltar kicked in. I'm sure internally he was a babbling lost soul, but only strength revealed itself to me. Except for the eyes. His eyes always speak truth to me.

He is torn by circumstance of worrying about me and his commitment to his job as an aircraft dispatcher for a major airline. I am in crisis, but he is supposed to be in a meeting with the FAA in just a few hours, a meeting he absolutely can't miss. He sits by my side as long as he can and then hesitantly says goodbye. He slips taxi money into my hand, hoping I'll be set free, but not trusting Seth to be there to take me home.

I grow frightened with his leaving, not sure what is going to happen next. I know that I'll be evaluated for mental stability as soon as the doctors arrive at 8 am.

Seth later remarked about how callus it was of Jeff to "desert me" when I needed him. "How rude to give you money for a taxi and then leave you," he said.

Jeff knew that the hospital, not Seth, ultimately controlled my fate. He trusted I would be okay. Still, I trusted nobody but Jeff. I was forced to trust the hospital because I couldn't escape it. I knew I had to control myself if I had any chance of regaining my freedom.

After my organ functions return to normal and my physical health is no longer in question, they move me to a holding room in the psych ward. The room is more like a jail cell, with cinderblock walls; thick, heavily scratched Plexiglas windows; and a thin foam mattress on a steel frame bolted to the wall. Ray drops in to continue screwing with my mind, telling me how crazy I have become and insisting that the doctors will know it. He too has that look of private pleasure, so I just bite my lip and endure the attack until he leaves. He is so much more powerful than me, I feel helpless in the face of his covert attack. I don't want to do anything to bring any attention to myself. I don't want to get trapped here. So I remain silent.

After showering and dressing for work, Jeff returns for one more quick visit. I tell him a little of what Ray said. Incensed, he immediately goes to the nurses and insists that neither Ray nor Seth be allowed to see me.

After he leaves, I try my best to rest. A genuinely crazy man is roaming around looking for an escape route, yelling and babbling nonsense about the world around him. The attending nurses, probably used to his craziness, show little compassion while tackling him to restrain him, which frightens me even more. I curl up in the corner and sob, begging God not to let this become my world.

I drift off to sleep before I hear the keys and clanging of the heavy steel door opening. It is the doctor. He introduces himself and then sits in the chair he has brought with him and quietly reads through my file. His calm presence does little to ease my fear and nervousness. This is the moment of truth that will decide the fate of my freedom. After about 10 minutes of questions, he determines that I am sane and no threat to myself. I assure him I will resume my therapy with Michael, and with that, he immediately discharges me and directs me to the nearest exit.

"Oh, thank you, God. I promise I will never do this again," I say quietly as I move toward the exit.

As I walk through the doors that lead into the waiting area of the ER, I see Seth and Ray sitting, quietly talking out their plan together. They look surprised when they see me defiantly walking up to them. I smile as I stand in front of them.

"What are you doing?" Seth asks. He is angry.

"I've been discharged. Let's go home." They are in shock. This confirms my fear that they wanted me committed, though I don't understand why. I know there is much about what is happening that I still don't understand. And I know I have to keep it together.

"What did you say to them?" Ray yells as quietly as he can without bringing attention to us. "I want to talk to the doctor!"

I look at them with unveiled disdain, armed with the full support of that doctor, and say, "We're leaving, now!"

As we walk out the emergency doors, it is like watching two idiot keystone cops trying to figure out what went wrong. They are so pissed off I think they are going to spontaneously combust. I notice my car and realize Seth felt comfortable enough to begin taking over my belongings while I was locked away.

The ride home is painfully silent but thankfully short. Back in the apartment, I immediately go to my room and slam the door. Seth and I haven't shared a room since the last time he wrapped his hands around my neck. Anger grows in me the more I think about their attempt to capitalize on my mental break. What else could explain their behavior during the past 24 hours? It seems they really wanted me to be locked away. I could only wonder why. Did Seth want to take possession of all my belongings, or was there some greater motive only he knew about? It couldn't be about something as silly as material possessions. I knew it had to be something much greater.

I hear them talking in the living room, so I quietly approach my bedroom door and strain to listen. As usual, they are talking too low for me to understand much, but I clearly hear Seth angrily reply to Ray, "Shut up, bitch, I'm high." Judging from their anger at my release, I think they are arguing about their failed mission.

I sit and think about everything that has happened and wonder what I should do next. I call Michael and leave a brief message about what happened and ask him to call me. Next, I start looking at my finances, knowing I have to move out of this hell I am in. Having been driven to such a desperate act, any illusions of personal safety have vanished. As I plan, I can hear them whispering in the other room, and it makes me angry. In a final dramatic huff that consumes my last ounce of energy, I bust out into the living room and inform both of them that as soon as I find a new place to live, I will be moving and Seth had better plan for it. I then return to my room, slam the door, climb into bed, and immediately drift into a deep long sleep.

Over the next couple of weeks, life returned to a somewhat normal routine. Though Seth and I didn't entirely come back together, the anger cooled and we drew closer again. This was so typical for us, almost an expected outcome of any argument, no matter how severe or damaging. Amazingly, I still felt much love for him, and he moped around in a depressed misery of apparent heartbreak himself. One afternoon, after he had been in bed for days, I joined him in his room and sat next to him on his bed, attempting to cheer him up. He just sobbed and started talking about ending his life. I don't know if he was serious or just playing with my emotions, but I grew alarmed and called Michael. He gave me some advice on what to look for and who to call for help, but the crisis quickly passed without event.

We no longer slept together and we defined ourselves as "just friends." He asked me to consider staying in the apartment with him until the lease was up, strictly as roommates, and foolishly, I wondered if maybe I could. It was going to cost $3000 to break the lease, an expense I'd surely bear alone. We brainstormed how we would handle such an arrangement, the awkwardness of seeing other people and various other situations that might arise. I asked him specifically not to ever sleep with anyone in my bed. I don't remember why, but it was a request I felt I needed to make.

The following Friday, on my way home from work, Seth calls me. He is really angry because Ricky, a neurotic friend of the group who is always high on crystal, had dropped by without calling first. Initially I don't understand why he is so angry. It is Friday afternoon, and he was just sleeping. What is there to be so angry about? When I arrive, they are smoking crystal and visiting, the way normal people might visit over coffee, and I see no visible sign of hostility. It doesn't make any sense, so I figure Seth has gotten over it, probably the moment Ricky pulled out the free Tina. Hooked into their life and lifestyle, I join them and a short time later Ricky leaves.

Seth invites me to attend a show that his performance group is hosting that evening, so we get ready and leave. Because he had volunteered to chauffeur the group, they provided an SUV for him to drive. On the road, he asks me to remind him to wash my sheets when we get home. When I ask why, he says he had an "accident" when he was napping in my bed that afternoon. From the look on his face, I understand clearly everything that has transpired earlier that day. I am speechless, my heart broken. As I stare out the passenger window, hiding my shock, I know it is time to move away from him.

I considered moving within the building to a one-bedroom to keep from breaking my lease, but I no longer felt safe living there. I knew my privacy was being invaded and moving to another unit would do little to escape that. With my trust of anything around me at an all-time low, I wasn't sure what to do.

Out of the blue, Benjamin, a friend I'd known before Seth, called. Benjamin and I had originally met in the same chat room that brought Seth into my life. As with most introductions that happen among guys who frequented that chat room, Benjamin and I started off as sex buddies, but after just a week, ours morphed into friendship. We hadn't spoken for some time and I was happily surprised to hear from him. We chatted for a while, catching up on each other's lives, and I eventually told him about my drama and current predicament. Guess what? He needed a roommate!

He lived in a rented house with his now ex-boyfriend and another friend. Because their relationship had ended, the boyfriend was moving out, so Benjamin invited me to move in. The rent was cheap, and he said I could move in the following month. I instantly knew this was the lucky break I had wished for and I gladly accepted his offer.

Back on top of my world, I immediately started planning for the move. I gave notice and begrudgingly handed over the check for $3000. Seth wasn't at all happy about my good fortune and tried everything he could think of to change my mind. He told me that Benjamin couldn't be trusted and that I was making a big mistake. It didn't work though and in no time I was packing boxes for the move. Though I was very happy about moving in with Benjamin, it was still heartbreaking to know I was leaving Seth. The contrast of the situation had me up and down like Tom Cruise on Oprah's couch.

Moving day was arduous, physically and emotionally. Tina and I stayed up the night before packing together, which didn't help my emotional strength at all. Tina was my only friend now. Whenever I was alone, as I often was now, I shared my time with Tina. I didn't feel alone when I was with Tina. Jeff, his friend Chris, and his boyfriend Dominic came to help with the move. Seth and Ray stopped by to make one last attempt to change my mind. Seth was high and so was I, so needless to say, it didn't proceed very amiably. Reaching a boiling point, I finally had to force him to leave. But the depression he caused stayed. This made the rest of the move miserable for me.

As much as I wanted to be closing the book on this painful chapter of my life, the truth was that Seth still held the reins to my heart and this move would do little to change that. Our relationship was in no way coming to an end because of this move, and the worst of the story had yet to play out. I still loved him and I still believed that he loved me, and that believing held me captive. I knew the drugs and drama were getting in our way. Privately, I thought the distance would calm this down. But I also feared he would let go of me, something I didn't want, even though I was the one walking away.

He's Back

Living with Benjamin began well enough. It was fun to have a friend I trusted to hang out with. There was a silliness to our friendship that brought me some temporary happiness. He had a lot of friends who seemed completely disconnected from the world I was trying to escape, so there was much to distract me from the enormous void this breakup was leaving in my life. It didn't really occur to me at the time as it does now, but the social fears I've suffered under for so many years weren't having as strong a spell over me. My monster seemed to have gone into hiding. I still got, and get, nervous around people in general, but somewhere along the way that fear had begun to loosen its grip over me.

At the same time, and almost immediately after moving, a new torture began. The first time, I was lying in bed trying to fall asleep. The sounds were as quiet as you could imagine, almost not there, like turning the volume down on the television to the lowest setting. But I knew I could hear Seth screaming in anger. He was yelling at someone, telling them how much he hated me and wanted to kill me.

"I hate that little fucker! I hate him! I want to kill him! I'm going to kill him! I hate him! Let me kill him! I want to kill him! I fucking hate him!" On and on it went. *Oh boy, David, you need to get some sleep.* Little did I know but this was just the beginning of a torment that would take center stage in the attempt to drive me out of my mind.

Within a few weeks Seth slowly worked his way back into my world. I think the voices frightened me into running back to him. Or maybe it was the loneliness of not having him next to me. I hated to be alone. Somewhere along the way I abandoned all separation from him and declared him once again my man. *Whitney has nothing on me, baby.* He'd even stay the night at my new place, something that made Benjamin boil over with anger. His hatred of Seth eventually proved terminal to our roommate situation, but not before much drama. I had become the Queen of Drama during those times, a title I abhorred once I held the crown. It was no longer a silly joke to be royalty of that nature. Drama had always been trivial to me, just gossip and giggles that people shared to entertain themselves. This drama was something I could have never imagined.

Seth now lived in a basement apartment near Ray. With summer returning to the Hill, the carefree partying we'd known in the beginning returned as well. But the clock couldn't be turned back on all that had happened nor could the effects of it be removed from my psyche. Ray believed differently. He continually deduced that my mind was "deleting files" whenever I got lost in his mind games. I think he confidently believed I was doing this with every memory I had, mostly because he did everything he could to confuse my mind during those days. But since I've been away from all of them, and all of that, I have been able to put the pieces back together again.

While assembling at Seth's apartment one night before heading out to the clubs, something peculiar happened. In a flash, I transformed into a hound dog who'd located a scent. With my spine stiff and nose out, I was on the hunt. We were typically all very high, Tina, Ellen, and Gina flowing through our systems. I became locked onto that same look I'd seen in Seth that night in the hospital. I had now learned to recognize it in Ray. As everyone milled about Seth's apartment, I suddenly recognized the tell-tale signs in others. It was easy to decode. Like a boy who just found Waldo in every collage of every book, I couldn't keep my eyes from gazing at the secret. I didn't realize it, but Seth was realizing that I was realizing. By then, most everyone else had departed, but Seth, Ray, and I remained. They were across the room, talking quietly and observing me. I excused myself to run to my car to get some gum and to give myself a moment to process data. When I returned, the energy toward me had shifted 180°. They had a genuine look of dread in their eyes, a frightened preoccupation that instantly changed everything. Ricky and Richard returned from next door and we started walking down the street toward the club. A private conversation transpired between all but me, and then everyone shared the same look of introverted melancholy.

Ray was singing *a cappella*, as he often did when there was something on his mind he couldn't directly share. The verses of this tune, "You found out … there's nothing going on … da da da … he found out … there's nothing going on" were sung as if he knew I had discovered something. This continued off and on until we arrived at the club. It was clear that they knew that I knew something was going on. For the rest of the night, the group kept a noticeable distance from me, continuing that look of worry, along with much crestfallen private talk. Others in the club, people I didn't even know, watched with the same heavy presence. It all took a toll on me. Seth was very quiet and seemed unusually worried and distant. He had this way about him when he was worried. He tried to carry on like nothing was wrong, casually bouncing around to the beat, but looking around with a foreboding that spoke volumes.

All at once, it became too much to bear, and I bolted. I just left. Too much whispering, too much distance, too many strange stares. I knew something was wrong and I didn't want to be alone in the air of it all. I ran to my car and drove home. How my just looking upon and understanding a piece of their truth could cause such a reaction was very troubling to me. Is it possible that somehow that event, my thoughts, their thoughts, all that had happened could be understood and witnessed by someone else or something else that I was unaware of? Like in *Lord of the Rings*, could some evil force be watching all of us? That night introduced a new layer of lead blanket that remained and, to some extent, remains today. Was I a living witness to something that is bigger than any secret that's ever been kept? A secret that reaches beyond our world, one that steps through a checked doorway into another? In my heart, I know the true answer is yes.

Exiled

Seattle Gay Pride 2003. Parades, parties, and celebrations. Aside from that, it sucked. The idea of it sounded fun to a little boy on his way to Disneyland. To a little boy that never knew about all of this shit that was now part of his life. But that little boy died. The one who survives is the one who knows.

I arrived at Seth's and shared my drugs with him and Ray before we departed. Always the little boy down the street who shares his candy with the other kids he thinks of as friends. Maybe it was just a result of time, or the result of all that had happened. Maybe I somehow still believed they really were my friends. Maybe it was all of this. This recipe brought us close to each other. My discovery of their world was driving a wedge between us, even though we were discovering friendship. My perspective was different from theirs. We had no choice but to accept our differences and make the best of it.

During the Pride events, there was a noticeable attention to me and the T-shirt I had chosen to wear. Understanding my perspective, it seemed fitting to wear Benjamin's grey athletic T-shirt stamped with PORN STAR IN TRAINING. The looks of shock and awe that followed cemented my feeling that my life was being piped into the homes of many. I knew it was happening, but I knew I was helpless to stop it. I could only acknowledge it. That was all I could do. People were watching moments that should have been private but weren't. And believe me, I have indulged in some very sketchy, naughty private moments. Some of those were brought about in my search for Seth's truth, but much was driven by the raw drug-induced pursuit of self-pleasure. I was high and horny.

Our favorite club had now closed, caught up in the construction delays and hassles of their move to a new location. With this void, we found ourselves a bit lost for a fabulous club to call home. The location just off Broadway where the Mass events took place continued the Sunday Tea Dances, though they weren't nearly as popular. Other nights, we were forced to frequent the Cuff, a darker leather man-bar that was growing in popularity with the circuit scene.

As our weekend parties carried on, I continued to observe the story within the story. With those revealing moments in the hospital, and all of my experiences with Seth and his world guiding me, I continued watching. I had amassed many "files" that helped me to understand what I was looking for. I knew its pleasure, and I felt its pain. I could now recognize the look of its existence. I had developed a sixth sense for it. I knew the truth.

Over the next weeks, I realized my presence in the clubs was no longer welcome. I instantly picked up on the hostility in the air whenever we were there. On the dance floor, I'd look around into the faces around me, and know they wanted to hurt me. I could see the loathing in their eyes, as though I were looking into the eyes of an army of devil's advocates who longed to plunge their talons into my throat and rip me apart. I didn't understand why, though I assumed it was because I was discovering their secrets. And knowing what I knew, I couldn't stop my pursuit. I had to know what it was that I was discovering. I sensed it was big, and important, too important for me to give up and run away.

Mornings were now spent at a new club in Pioneer Square, our hangout since the closing of Bananas. But now, rather than eagerly pouring ourselves through the door, we often held back and just gathered outside. Hesitant to step inside, a sense of alarm would suddenly overtake our reckless high. It seemed mutual, like we were staying outside because we all felt abruptly unsure about stepping inside and disappearing into the dark caverns of the private club that had before been such a welcome playground. What exactly that danger was, I wasn't sure, but I sensed it wasn't anything I wanted to know. After milling about on the sidewalk for a while, someone would finally say to the group, "I'm not really sure I want to go in. How about you?"

Everyone quickly agreed. The others spread the word and we all journeyed back to our cars and headed in a new direction. But the heaviness of what had happened stayed with us.

It's hard to explain all the idiosyncrasies that formed the setting of any given moment in that time. As I was kept in the dark about so much, most often the only things I had to go by were my history, the subtle body language I'd grown to understand, and the cryptic messages of everyone around me. It was obvious that I was the only one who was ignorant, and I struggled to understand why. Very few outside our innermost group talked to me anymore, and most around us just looked upon me with a guarded curiosity. So much about all of this seemed impossible, but at the same time, it was wrapped in a layer of reality. It was truly a journey through the Twilight Zone. I know today if I were to be plopped into the same situation, I'd know in an instant that I had just fallen down the rabbit hole, and I would know exactly what to do. I wish I had then.

It's early Sunday and we are hovering around the entrance to Larry's. I noticed Dan, the doorman, talking with Shelly, a friend of Fred's. They are fixed on me while they are talking. The seriousness makes me feel worried. Shelly has always been very nice to me; I've never seen this look in her eyes. I roam around casually until I'm within earshot of their conversation, pretending not to notice them. I hear him say to her as they stare at me, "His days are numbered." Sadness washes over her face. I know she has just heard the same sentence I did. I quickly move away, feigning ignorance as to what has just happened, hoping to not blow my cover.

After several of these episodes, I grew to know that I was in some serious trouble. I was a blind man in a dark room looking for a black cat that wasn't there. Then how was I to find it?

By now, it was extremely troubling for me to go out because I couldn't keep from picking up on the dark vibrations that surrounded me wherever we went. The negative energy would cause me to spiral into a quiet, despondent isolation. The cloak of wallflower that had always protected me whenever I needed to escape into anonymity was failing me now. I would often resort to hiding in bathroom stalls for a few minutes time just to escape the anxiety that would engulf my mind. One of the last times Seth and I went out together, he invited along a friend of his, someone who worked at the University of Washington. It seemed strange that this guy was tagging along with us because he didn't seem the partying type. I had the sense he was there to bear witness to what was happening, to the hostility, and also to keep us safe. That night, there was an intense rancor in the air, and Seth seemed particularly worried. I realized that if this guy hadn't been with us, something bad would have happened.

Because of all of this, our weekends drifted away from the clubs, and more to just hanging out at Seth's or other homes of those within our immediate circle. The music and socializing that was signature to our glamorous world became off-bounds. I think that contributed to the increased arguing between Seth and me, and our increasing isolation from his party world. Ray stayed away now, hardly ever going out. Seth said it was because he and Richard were fighting a lot. I found myself drifting away from their world, spending more time at home with Benjamin.

Then came Canada.

Vancouver BC Pride 2003

When Seth first started talking about the Rapture 4 Pride weekend, I didn't plan on going. He had attended the previous August, before we met, with several members of his group and had really enjoyed it. I could tell it had had a profound effect on him because he raved about it so much. He had shown me pictures from the weekend and described the events many times.

There was this one snapshot of him that stuck with me. It didn't seem so unusual to me back then, but now I better understand why he made such a point of it. Wearing shorts and a tank, he was dripping from head to toe in sweat, except for the triangle of his crotch. That was completely dry. It was clear in observing the photo, the way it captured his purposeful attention to the dry area of his groin, that the motive was to capture the peculiarly dry spot. He showed it to me several times, trying to relate to me his bewilderment about it. "Isn't that strange?" he'd say. It seemed strange to me that this picture caused such a commotion in him, but I smiled and replied, "Wow, that is strange!" Today, I understand.

I grumbled that I didn't want to go, but he was swift and forceful in persuading me to change my mind.

"Oh, you have to go. It's so much fun!"

"But Seth, I don't feel comfortable. You know what it's like when we go out. We just fight and people don't like it. I don't want to ruin it for everyone else. I don't want to go."

He insisted, raving about all the incredible fun we would have. He went on and on about the clubs, especially The World. "You must go to The World."

"But Seth, you know how much we fight. It's not a good idea. Everyone will get mad at us. Please, I don't want to go."

After endless arm-twisting, I finally agreed to go. Once the decision was made, I became excited about it, looking forward to all that he had told me about. I went online and ordered a bunch of circuit party favors for everyone: T-shirts, flashing lights, mini glow sticks, temporary tattoos, socks, I bought it all. I even ordered these six little stuffed bears in rainbow colors with the intention of making a statement when I handed them out to the group. I'm sure that didn't help my situation at all.

When Benjamin found out I was going, he blew a gasket! He begged me not to go.

"They are going to hurt you, David. You can't go."

"Oh, come on. Nobody's going to hurt me."

"Yes they are. They are going to kill you."

He did everything he could to persuade me to back out. Seth said that he was just trying to "sketch" me out and I should ignore him.

"Benjamin is a drama queen. He just screws with you because he knows it works. You can't let him get to you."

After realizing he'd failed to convince me to stay, Benjamin started warning me about the trip. He said there would be "clocks."

"There will be clocks. Watch the clocks, David. The clocks will have different times. Time will go forward and backward. Watch the clocks." That's all he would say. Okay, maybe I thought he was just trying to screw with my head.

The Thursday night before we left was filled with fighting and madness. I had to work Friday, so I was home packing my bags, getting things ready before I turned in for the night. Seth was starting his party early, flying on Tina. By now, I understood how different he could be when he was high. Sober, he was a mellow, peaceful guy. High on Tina, he became hell-bent on fighting with me about anything, condemning me for the way I exhaled. I don't think he was really aware of the effect meth had on his personality. I tried to show it to him, but he never got it or just refused to admit it.

On this night, he was flipping out because he couldn't find his passport. He had ripped his apartment to pieces to no avail. I figured he was just high and sketchy, so I encouraged him to calm down to clear his head. Oh, he was having none of that. Before I knew it, we were screaming at each other, hanging up, calling back, text-messaging, furiously arguing the way we did. It was so pathetic. You've never seen anybody text message with the adeptness we developed during that relationship. And you've probably never known anybody who broke up via text messaging as much as we did. It didn't matter if we were at the club, on the dance floor, or in the bathroom, there we'd be texting away, breaking up and making up on stage for everyone to see.

After giving into him, I got into my car and quickly drove to his place. When I arrived, he was high and messy. I watched him rip everything apart in his meth-crazed tantrum, looking for his passport. I tried to calm him down, but he just kept going.

To end the madness, I yelled, "I'm not going!"

He looked at me like he wanted to kill me and yelled, "Yes, we are!"

"Wow," I yelled back. "I can't wait to go! Good night!" I walked out, slamming the door behind me.

He called me repeatedly.

Knowing I couldn't go to work sketchy, I turned my phone off and went to bed. He eventually found his passport and the next day apologized for everything. Kiss-kiss, I love you. All was well in our sick little world.

Out of nowhere, Seth suggested I rent a car. He said it would be better than taking both of our cars. Until then, he had refused, wanting to take two cars.

Rather than argue, I said, "Yes, dear." After work, I picked up the car, swung by my place to grab my bags, and then drove to Seth's. That's when he told me Ray wouldn't be going. And that was the wrong answer for me. There is no way Ray wasn't going with us.

I knew he absolutely had to go with us. I had little trust in Seth at this point, and less in Ray, but it was more than I had in any of the others. For some reason, I knew I needed Ray to be with us. Was it intuition? I don't know. But he proved instrumental to my coming home alive. After begging Ray with every ounce of guilt I could muster, he hesitantly gave in.

While he packed, Seth sent me to fetch Kurt. I helped him pack his many bags of toys, lights, and sparkly circuit stuff. Kurt was a strange one. But Seth kept him close, like a distant family member. An hour and half later, we finally arrived back at Seth's, loaded their bags, and hit the highway. We did what Tina we had before we left, making sure to not have any drugs on our persons as we passed through the border. For some reason, everyone was afraid to take drugs across the border, so Heyden had placed our orders with dealers he knew in Vancouver. I wondered why everyone was suddenly so afraid. On our last journey to Vancouver together, we had carried plenty of drugs over the border with us.

No sooner than we'd journeyed beyond the city limits of Seattle did the sketch begin. Seth immediately distanced himself from me, focusing all of his attention on the others. When I tried to bring myself into the conversations, he would talk over and ignore me. Kurt seemed to be enjoying this. And even though we were listening to music through the car stereo, Ray chose to put on headphones and remove himself from the atmosphere of the car altogether. He initially didn't want to go to Canada, and now he was doing his best to separate himself from everything that was happening. This was so unlike Ray. Usually he was the center of attention.

At Kurt's request, we put in a CD he had burned especially for the trip. The only song I remember was "Fire" by Dolce, probably because this song was repeated many times during the 3-hour ride to Vancouver. The lyrics had a profound and intentional effect on the mood of the trip. The song is hardcore prose filled with anger toward someone who had supposedly lied to, cheated on, and backstabbed his significant other. It is a classic jilted-lover song, but with a message of impending revenge, a message I began to believe was intended for me. Because of this song, I feared I really was headed for trouble on this trip, just as Benjamin had tried to warn me about.

About halfway there, we stopped at McDonald's for a bathroom break and some dinner. Nobody was talking to me now. I went about ordering my food and then waited for everyone else. Kurt, Seth, and Ray disappeared into the bathroom. A lot of secret talk was going on. It was pointless to try to eavesdrop; all I could do was know it was happening. I remember wanting to jump into the car, peel rubber, and leave them there. I wanted to run home and get away from them. I almost talked myself into doing it, but they reappeared before I made my move. Instead, we piled back into the car and continued our journey.

Wonderland

When we finally arrive at our hotel in Vancouver, as we are collecting our bags from the car, Seth informs me that it would be best for me to check into the room without mentioning that anyone else is with me.

"Tell me you're not serious?" I say.

"We'll save money this way."

"We?" *Who the hell are "we"? I'm the dumb ass paying for everything. You brought me here to hurt me; you can at least pay for my room!* Yes, even though I didn't start off wanting to join them on this trip, I ended up paying for it.

After arguing back and forth, Kurt reluctantly agrees to be on the bill, though I doubt he will pay for anything. He stands off to one end of the counter during check-in, so who knows what really transpired. I never saw his name printed on anything. After receiving the keys, Kurt goes outside to collect everyone. We all pile into the elevator together, with little concern that anyone will realize we are together. And other than the stares from the employees and shady looking guests in the lobby, nobody says anything to us.

After settling into the room, I try to relax for a bit to calm my nerves. Later, we primp for our first night out on the town. By now, I am feeling alone in the lions' den. Heyden and Brad show up with drugs and a few other people, strangers only to me. After distribution, we snort, bump, swallow, and smoke. Following the theme already set by the drive up, I am included in little of the conversation. I don't feel like I am in immediate danger, but I keep thinking about the warnings Benjamin had tried to give me. So I become a silent detective, pretending nothing is wrong but carefully processing everything that is happening, hoping to figure out what lies ahead.

Our first night at the clubs is surprisingly fun. Once we step out into the nightlife, the dark heaviness lifts enough to allow me to break from the paranoia and have some fun. This night's destination is the World, the club Seth couldn't talk enough about. It is within walking distance of our hotel but further down into a seedier part of town. From the street it looks like the entrance to a large gothic movie theater, but after passing through the long row of glass doors, the room beyond is empty except for a discreet staircase in the back corner that leads down into the basement where the club is.

It turns out to be one large room with a low ceiling that you could almost reach up and touch, packed with people dancing and milling about. There's a coat check, dance floor, DJ booth, back bar, and a smaller "chill" room off to the back for lounging, typical of many clubs like this. Filled with hypnotic trance music, dim red lighting, and deep sofas, this room provides a sexy, dark, somewhat secluded area for those partaking in drugs and "other" influences to relax and enjoy the ride. A snapshot would have revealed faces filled with a rapturous energy you'd only expect from someone reveling in the glorious moments of climax, not fully dressed people sitting around socializing at a nightclub. To the untrained eye, this might appear a room filled with people enjoying their chemical high, for the untrained, unenlightened eye wouldn't know the look of "the secret."

Seth and I remain alone for most of the night. Ray and the others scatter and rarely make an appearance. As we dance and mingle, I start to notice a change in Seth's behavior. Knowing full well what's going on, I quickly grow frustrated and angry. But when he starts to lose control of himself, I become concerned. What starts off as a look of private pleasure turns into a crippling agony that grows in intensity as the night progresses. Seth is doubling over and grabbing at his stomach as though he is having intense cramps. But this pain seems to be out of his control, caused by forces outside of his body. The more intense it becomes, the more his desperate eyes search around until his attention becomes fully focused on the DJ booth.

Pulling me with him, he hobbles us in front of the booth and resorts to hanging off of it, groaning in pain and glaring at the DJs with an unmistakable look of duress. There is a look of pleading in his face as he moves back and forth in front of the DJs, begging for their attention. They doggedly keep their eyes from meeting his, and as their hands move about the various buttons on their control board, Seth's contractions and moanings seem choreographed to those movements.

I stand back in dumbfounded shock as I watch them dance him around like some puppet. Not believing what I am witnessing, I search around us for help that isn't there. Everyone seems to be enjoying what is happening; they look satisfied with the punishment being inflicted upon Seth. Punishing him for allowing me to discover the secrets they hold. I am high, suddenly alone, and unimaginably afraid of where I am. Seth is on the verge of passing out and I feel like hungry wolves surround me.

Finally, the music stops and so does Seth's struggling, though it takes him a while to collect himself. I was never so happy to reach the closing moments of a night at the club. As the lights slowly brighten, Seth calms down and we go in search of our friends. I know not to say a word about what I've witnessed, so I just focus my attention on locating Ray and making sure Seth is okay.

Once our group has collected, we somberly walk back to the hotel and chill for a while. More than ever before, I know I am caught up in something more bizarre and dangerous than I could have ever imagined.

After sunrise, when regular people once again filled the streets of Vancouver, the three of us embarked upon some wide-eyed sightseeing of our own. Though I initially felt like the unwanted child being lugged around on some suburban mommy's shopping adventure, I later realized I was the star attraction of the day's blockbuster. Seth and Ray held many war-room whispering sessions, but that's not what was so unordinary about the day. While at first it seemed like the careless wanderings of sketchy shopping, in and out of the many shops and boutiques of Granville, I soon realized there was much more happening below the surface. The world shrank dramatically for me during that day, revealing hidden layers of a collective consciousness I never could have imagined.

Ray seemed to be on a mission that both disturbed and enchanted me. As they whisked me in and out of the stores, I realized he was going to great efforts to get noticed by the CCTV cameras in each store, positioning himself, and us in front of them, and performing wildly. He obnoxiously made our presence known. Whether it was running into people, knocking displays over, or just plain silly, impromptu stunts, Seth and Ray seemed determined to get us noticed, with Ray undeniably commanding the Oscar. I don't know if Seth had the same intention for Ray was the lead character of this act. As we exploded out the door and into strangers on the street, Ray would accost whoever was around and flamboyantly ejaculate, "Hello! [Big gay smile] Thanks for watching." Then he'd introduce his cracked-out posse and entreat them to snap our picture, followed by a scandalously hilarious compliment about their "sweater," a schizophrenic burst of insincere sofa talk, then whoosh, he'd whisk us off to our next performance. This act repeated itself throughout the day. Our behavior was absolutely committable. Surely we could have been arrested, but oddly, I don't think any shop owner wanted that for us. Many of them grinned and encouraged our performance with enthusiasm. In the beginning, I assumed Ray was just entertaining our high, but with each passing hour, I knew something more important was unfolding. I just couldn't figure out what.

Then it hit me. He wanted people to recognize us and remember meeting us. I didn't understand his reasons, but I began playing along, mostly because it was insanely amusing. But it felt significant too. I had a sense I was helping myself, that all of this was because of me. Ray and I had a way of playing our silly humor off each other, and this day provided the greatest audience for our shenanigans. It was all fun enough, but by the afternoon, I noticed something ominous that quickly unsettled me. It seemed nearly everyone around us now, whether in a store or on the street, recognized us and was aware of what we were doing. And nearly every other face in the crowd seemed unhappy about it. Young, old, rich, poor, it didn't matter. The collective knew something. The flames that burned in their angry eyes chilled my spine. The excitement I was enjoying suddenly vanished, replaced by a cold, lonely fear.

While all this was happening, I began showing signs of some sort of physical attack. My right eye was mysteriously developing what might have been a bad case of pink eye, but it seemed more than that to me. By evening, it became blood red with puss oozing from it in a constant messy flow. I eventually lost muscle control around the eye, so the upper and lower lids hung slack. I've had pink eye before but never anything like this. Seth and Ray didn't say much about it, other than suggesting I keep my sunglasses on. The way they would look at each other with such sadness caused me to think they knew something more about this than they were letting on. The fact that everyone kept silent about something so obviously wrong spoke loudly to me. Nobody ever said a word about it. And that lack of concern told me that whatever was happening with my eye, that should be the least of my worries. That was the moment when I first started to believe that I might not live through the night. And in that moment of clarity, I understood just how screwed I was. I knew it would take a miracle to get me out of this situation.

With the sun giving way to a dark sky laced with crimson clouds, we made our last pass through the city before heading back to the room. As we passed in front of the World, I noticed a small pack of bodies dressed in full black coming up the opposite side of the street. Arm in arm, with one guy draped in a leather trench coat, insolently sucking on a cigar, they sauntered along, guffawing like royalty parading in front of lesser mortals. When they drew close, I realized they were all wearing the same black T-shirt, emblazoned with "Gambino Family Reunion 2003." I knew enough to know these people don't advertise, ever. I couldn't help but wonder why this was happening now.

Somewhere along the way, Seth picked up hair bleach, deciding to adopt my trademark platinum look as his own. Back in the room, Ray assumed the task of hairdresser and I entertained them, and myself, with music and lighthearted conversation. I was trying my best to pretend nothing was wrong. The contrast of emotions I was feeling is a hard mix to explain. There was a peaceful calm among the three of us, a strange fellowship in the midst of all this. I was eerily calm, enjoying our private little party together but also despondent about what was coming. Because of the day's earlier events, I felt an intense love for these two and this moment, but a silent dread was building somewhere deep within that I tried to pretend wasn't there. I felt solace even though I knew forces greater than me and invisible to me were soon going to deliver me to death's door, and nothing in this world was going to stop it from happening. I secretly wondered how it would happen as I pranced around the room, feigning indifference. Would my questions finally be answered? Would it be violent and gruesome, or would they allow me quietly to go to sleep? I wondered so much about that coming final moment.

I remember feeling a deep love for Seth. I knelt on the floor in front of him and lay my head in his lap while Ray attended to his hair. There was a profound sadness in the room with us. They talked vaguely and morosely about something that was coming, something I understood, we all understood, silently together. I felt hopelessly trapped, so I wasn't resisting it. We were doing an unusually heavy amount of drugs that weekend, more than we'd ever done at one time, so that may have contributed to my calm acceptance. It seemed they wanted me to be really high. Did they think that maybe it wouldn't hurt as bad, or that I wouldn't fear it as much? I guess it was helping, as strange as that sounds. With all that had happened, before and after arriving in Vancouver, I knew it was impossible for me to escape the end that was slowly drifting toward me. I was in the midst of my swan song.

Seth talked defiantly about what he was going to do when he got back to Seattle. Not defiant to me, but aloud as if whatever forces that were responsible for this were listening. He made reference to never again trying to have a boyfriend. He would stop fighting and do what he was supposed to do.

"I'll give all those little fucking twinks what they deserve." He had so much anger toward twinks, as though he despised what they represented. Twink is gay slang to describe an attractive young or young-looking gay male. Seth had always displayed a jealous anger toward them. He went on to explain that this was just his life, alluding to being part of a "gay mafia" but also noting that he didn't get any money or other benefits from it. He did seem proud of himself though and relieved in his sudden candor. Ray didn't say much; he seemed cautious about his words and actions now.

Later that evening, Kurt returns with a few other people and all of us start readying ourselves to go out to the main event, Rapture, which was taking place at the Plaza of Nations. Just before we depart, I excuse myself and go to the bathroom. In a sudden flood of emotion, I start trembling and crying. I quickly turn on the water so nobody can hear me. I stare at myself in the mirror, looking at my swollen, saggy eye, and cry. Sensing I am nearing the end, I say goodbye to my family, telling each of them how much I love them and I pray to my mom, telling her I am coming to be with her.

Seth knocks on the door, so I quickly pull myself together, dry my face, put on my sunglasses, and with one last look at myself, I say goodbye, turn, and open the door. When I come out, everyone just stares at me like they know what has just happened. I then say, "Let's do it."

Before leaving the room, I suddenly remember the surprise gifts I brought with me. "Hold on. I've got something for everyone." I run to my suitcase and pull out the stuffed bears and hand one to each person. When Heyden asks what they are for, I say, "To attach to your waistband, silly."

"Where's yours?" Seth asks.

I defiantly look him in the eyes, then the others, and say, "I don't get one. I'm not part of the club."

They look around at each other uneasily, not really sure what to do or say. I'm sure this act of defiance doesn't help my situation much, but I'm not going out without speaking my mind. And with that, we leave.

It is very quiet during the cab ride to the Plaza. We arrive early, so there aren't many people there yet. We make our way inside and explore the huge venue that ultimately will hold tens of thousands. After milling about for a while, we settle into an area off to one side of the main dance floor. As we wait for more of our friends to arrive, we each take turns going to the bathroom to do more GHB. I am now fiercely on guard, watching and wondering when something bad is going to happen. I am also very suspicious of everyone and everything. I don't want to be left alone, so the idea of going to the bathroom alone scares the crap out of me. Seth knows I am afraid but begins to ridicule me in front of everyone, so I become angry and storm off. Alone in the bathroom, I start freaking out. Deciding against taking anymore Gina, fearing I will fall out, I quickly run back out, mostly to make sure they haven't left me. I am really afraid they are going to leave me in the hands of some unknown thugs. I have already decided that if I am going to die tonight, they are going to stand witness to it.

Realizing they are still there, I slow my pace and return to them. They stand around talking among themselves and I look off to the dance floor, watching the lights and listen to the music. As more and more of our people gather, I notice their uneasy stares and hushed conversations. Matt, one guy I trusted more than any of the rest because he had never really wronged me, arrives with a couple of strangers. I see him looking at me, so I walk up to him to say hi, but when I draw close, I realize there are tears running down his cheeks. He looks fiercely into my eyes and then gives me a long hard hug. He then grabs the attention of his friends and they quickly walk away without saying goodbye to anyone. Troubled by this, I walk off toward the dance floor and climb up onto a huge dancing box. As I wipe the tears from my eyes, I attempt to distract myself with the music and lightshow. Before long, I am dancing and pretending nothing bad is happening. I keep a close eye on Seth and Ray though, making sure they don't try to go anywhere.

By now it is getting pretty crowded. The black-and-white checkered main stage lights up and some performers begin assembling. It's then that I notice the mural on the wall behind the stage. It is a huge 20-foot drawing of a round clock. In the middle is a simple face with the right eye closed. When they start performing, I notice the lyrics are about a boy, saying this is wrong, he didn't know, it's not his fault, you can't do this to him. I know without a doubt that they are singing about me.

When I look at Seth and Ray, their expressions confirm what I know to be true. I suddenly become very excited that I have people on my side, people who are now speaking out to help me. I jump down off the box and tell them I want to get closer to the stage. At first Seth objects, but they follow when I take off anyway. Up closer now, I push my way through the crowd until I am just feet from the stage. I notice that there is a television crew on the stage, recording the performance. Occasionally the camera pans around at the crowd, and when it comes to me, I jump up and down so that I will be noticed.

I look over at Seth and Ray, and they appear confused and very pissed. I lean in close to Seth's ear and say, "This means I'm untouchable now, doesn't it?"

He looks at me with disbelief and screams, "WHAT DID YOU SAY?"

I yell back, "I said this means I'm untouchable now, doesn't it?"

He looks at Ray who is looking at us, then looks back at me, his face filled with rage, and says, "Yes, I guess it does." He then grabs my arm and they pull me back through the crowd away from the stage.

We stand off to the back of the crowd for a bit, while they frantically strategize. I am ecstatic about my sudden good fortune. People I recognize from the Seattle scene are now making appearances, some of whom approach me with smiles to say hi, or just pat me on the back and journey on. I can tell that they too understand what is happening, and for this brief moment I wonder if maybe some of those Seattleites might actually be rooting *for* me. Soon Seth pulls me by the arm and says we are going back to the room. Without realizing the mistake I am making, I go along without hesitation.

The three of us pile into a cab and start back to our hotel in Granville. They whisper a little, but with me sitting so close, they mostly sit quiet, their minds no doubt racing as to what to do next. The cab driver keeps looking at us through the rear view mirror, which stirs a sudden uneasiness in me. That's when I first realize I might have done something really stupid by leaving the Plaza.

As we turn left onto Granville Street, I notice what looks to be black armored military vehicles parked one after another, completely lining the four-block stretch between Dunsmuir and Nelson Street where the hotel is located. Standing at attention alongside each vehicle are armed police or military men, dressed in full black body armor, holding large rifles. The sidewalks are filled with people milling about, probably partiers and other not-so-well-intended people. All eyes follow our cab as we slowly make our way down Granville Street. The closer we get to the hotel, the more I know I have really screwed up by coming back here. We make another left onto Nelson and I look back at the armored cars, then to the mobs flanking the car and finally to Seth and Ray. As we pull up to the hotel, I tell Seth I want to go back to the Plaza.

Seth responds coldly, "Why?"

"Because my friends, people who know me, are there."

"Your friends? You don't have any friends," he says. "Go if you want to."

"I don't want to go alone. I want you to come with me."

"No. If you go back, you're going by yourself."

I take one more look at the driver, then around at all the shady characters lurking beyond. I glance up at Seth as he climbs out of the car, tosses me a dirty look, and walks away. Wasting no time, I jump out and quickly follow them into the hotel lobby. I know, without a doubt, if I drive off alone in that taxicab, it will be the last anyone ever sees of me.

As we make our way to the elevator, I notice that the men in the lobby gathered around the fireplace begin to move toward us, in a manner meant to intimidate. They look as "mafia" as any crowd I could imagine.

On this night, for the first time, the impossibly hidden dark forces, those behind all the unimaginable nightmarish events I'd experienced since meeting Seth on that fateful date nearly a year before, began to reveal themselves. Everything had culminated into this grand moment of near-perfect planning. I knew tonight was the night they would seek their horrific revenge on me for discovering their dark world of secrets, and I still couldn't figure out how to escape.

Back in the room, Seth stomps around in a huff while I hide in the bathroom, trying to figure out what to do next. When I come out, Ray is gone. Then comes a knock at the door, and when Seth opens it, two sinister-looking characters stroll in. My heart skips a beat and my face flushes, but Seth seems at ease. They carry on a conversation like they are old friends, though I'd never seen them before.

Seth pulls out his glass pipe and starts smoking some Tina. He passes it around to the other guys who smoke from it, and then one of them passes it to me. I hesitantly take it from his hand, then quickly start smoking, intending to inhale as much as my lungs can hold, as fast as I can get it in. I'd been awake for nearly three days now, and with the drugs leaving my system, fatigue had already begun washing over my body in waves. If I were to fall asleep, I knew that would be the end for me.

Frightened for my life, I intend to smoke every drop in the pipe but instead manage just a small puff. The pipe is empty.

After inhaling what I can, I hand the pipe back to the stranger who'd passed it to me. He goes into the bathroom and after a few minutes comes back out. He asks me if I want more, and I say yes. As I start smoking, I begin to choke, and he gets this malevolent grin on his face that instantly petrifies me.

When I hand it back to him, he smiles at Seth and starts rambling about the damage that super glue can cause to your lungs if you smoke it. They chuckle a little, and then he says he needs to clean the pipe out before he smokes any more. I fear I have gravely miscalculated that move.

Afterward, he loads it up with huge rocks of crystal and proceeds to smoke and smoke and smoke. The more he smokes, the more agitated he becomes. He seethes about "doing some damage" and alludes to something bad that is going to happen. I experience an unspoken freak-out and realize I have to get out of the room. I get up and walk to the door.

Surprised, Seth asks me where I am going, to which I flip back, "to look for Ray."

He demands I stay but I give him *that look* and slam the door behind me. I stand out there for a few minutes, but he doesn't pursue. I can't figure out whether this is good or bad, so I gulp down my fear and run.

I am in an incredibly intense state of anxiety, not unlike a soldier would experience in a war zone or a stalked animal fleeing for his life, every action and thought determined by life or death. I almost get into the elevator but then realize that it isn't safe, so instead I take the stairs. My fear and panic are peaking now. I know being alone is a stupid move, so I start to run down the stairs to the lobby. Then I hear the pounding of many feet coming up from below, so I panic and run back up to my floor. I can hear people running through the halls above and below me. I look up and down, and then to the stairwell. *Oh God, it's happening. Fuuuuuuuuuuck!*

I run back and forth looking for a way out. Then my inner mind yells, *Call someone, David!* Instantly, I pull out my phone. I know Jeff was in Europe, so I call Benjamin, the only person who knows where I am. The phone rings and rings and then goes to voicemail. I call again but nothing. I leave a panicked message, and then hang up. I scroll through my address book and realize I have nobody. Other than my family way off in Colorado, the only other numbers in my phonebook are Seth's friends.

Then I see Jan's name. She is a client I have done graphic design for. Over the years we had developed a friendship that transcended our work together. We'd occasionally had dinners together, and I'd been to her home a few times. Though I don't feel comfortable calling her at three am, high as I am on drugs, she seems the only person who can help me. So hesitantly I push send.

"Hi, Ted. Sorry to be calling so late. Can I please talk to Jan?"

"Dave, is that you?"

I quickly apologize for the late call and explain that I am in trouble and need her help. He wakes her and puts her on the phone.

I tell her I am in Vancouver with Seth and Ray and something bad is happening. As quickly as possible I share as much as I can. I ask her to call Benjamin. She asks where I am but I don't know. Being so frightened and sketchy, I can't remember names, locations, or any concrete detail about anything. I am scared out of my mind.

The elevator opens and Ray appears. Busted! His expression quickly changes to worry when he sees me on my phone.

"Who are you talking to?" he asks.

"A friend of mine, someone you don't know."

He runs into the room, and a few seconds later Seth flies out the door, storms up to me, and yells at me, "David, hang up that phone, NOW!"

"No."

"You'd better hang up that fucking phone, David."

Jan is getting alarmed now. I can hear her and her husband trying to figure out where I am. This goes on for a few minutes until Seth goes back into the room and slams the door. With a look of defeat, Ray sits on the stairs, holds his hand out, and asks if he can talk to her. She agrees, so I hesitantly hand the phone to him. They talk for a short while, he assuring her that everything will be okay. After telling her where we are and personally guaranteeing my safety, he hands the phone back to me. I can tell the balance of power has shifted to my favor, once again.

Jan is hesitant to believe him when I get her back on the phone, but I feel safer now that somebody I trust knows where I am and whom I am with, so I tell her I'll be okay. I promise to keep her posted throughout the night and until I get back home.

"Let's go back into the room," Ray says.

"I don't want to. I don't trust those people in there."

"Hmm. Well, let's go for a walk then."

"Ray, please promise me nothing is going to happen to me."

"Just stay with me."

As we walk out of the hotel, the same shady characters in the lobby stand up and watch us go. On the street, more of the same. They are everywhere.

Ray stands in front of me and says, "Stay close behind me and don't allow anyone to come between us. If anyone tries anything, let me handle it."

We make our way down Granville, dodging anyone who comes close. Angry faces curse us and bully us as they pass, but Ray shows an equal force, ultimately keeping everyone at bay. It was unbelievable.

After walking several blocks of this war zone, we finally sit down and take refuge in front of a well-lit hotel entrance. There we sit in silence and rest. I ask Ray what is going on, but he doesn't say anything. He just stares at me. I can see that he is extremely worried. I figured he was probably in trouble for helping me.

Because of my eye and what that guy had said about the super glue, I ask, "Is there already something inside me that is going to kill me?"

"I'm not sure." He seems sincere.

"Maybe I should go to the emergency room?"

"No, we can't trust it. I think we need to go back to the room. It's too dangerous to be out here alone like this."

On the way, we stop by a store to get something to drink. We are both dehydrated and extremely thirsty. Everywhere we turn though, we are faced with hostility. It doesn't seem to matter if we are on the street or in a store, the glares and stares we receive let us know that we are not safe. I stay close to Ray as he pushes his way through various groups of menacing faces that cross our path, each seeming to be looking for an opportunity to make a move.

As we continue walking with bottled water in hand, Ray warns me not to drink anything from the faucets in the room or from any open containers.

"Do you think they will try to poison me?"

"I don't know what they are going to do. You can't take any chances, okay?"

"Okay."

The last few blocks of the walk feel particularly perilous to me, something that isn't lost on Ray either. He grows increasingly apprehensive at any shadowy moves around us. At one point when we both notice some shady characters climbing out of a car to our left, he tells me to run as fast as I can to the hotel if they attack us. They watch us for what feels like forever, but they don't make a move.

When we get back to the room, several other people are there, including Kurt. Seth is a total bitch towards me, putting me down and making me the butt of his mean-spirited jokes, with his entourage laughing in clear support. I stay silent and sit close to Ray. It is clear that everyone is upset with my apparent luck, and they aren't happy with Ray's actions to protect me.

They are all primping to go to the last event, the Rapture Recovery at the Beatty Street Armoury. Seth goes on and on about the Armoury as a place where bullets could fly and bodies could fall and no one would notice. He is obviously trying to frighten me again, and it is working. I have no reason to believe that any of what he says isn't possible or inevitable.

Ray says he isn't going, and with that I am happy to say I will stay with him. But then he and some of the others start talking in a way that makes me believe something is going to happen to us if we stay in the room.

"Ray, you really shouldn't stay here with him. Why don't you come with us?" Kurt says.

"Fuck it! I don't care what happens now. What's done is done."

"You're stupid if you stay," Seth says.

"Fuck you, Seth. Don't you get it? I'm done. It doesn't matter if I stay or go. I'm tired of this shit."

"Whatever, Ray. Be stupid then."

Before long, I have the feeling that Ray and I both are going to suffer the same fate. Seth again pleads with Ray to go to the Armoury with them. I have resigned myself to doing whatever Ray wants, because he has become the only person I feel any trust for, even if it means we are going to die together. I know my fate is out of my hands now. Escape seems impossible to me. Somehow I don't fear the end as much knowing that Ray is going to be there with me. It's strange to say, but just as earlier in the evening, that same sense of fellowship has returned, though Seth is not included now.

It's quiet for a while. After some intense thinking, Ray unexpectedly decides that we will go to the Armoury. Thinking he must have figured a way out, I become hopeful. Though the physical and emotional strain is taking its toll on me, I can't let my guard down for a moment. My only hope is that Ray will get us out of this. I have been diminished to a wild-eyed animal fearing imminent death. Every thought, every action is focused on the sole purpose of survival. Life no longer holds any gray areas for me; there are just black-and-white, yes-or-no decisions determined by life or death.

Just before leaving, everyone drinks down a G-tini, everyone but Ray and me. To my surprise, mine is already poured and waiting. Cheers to the dead man walking!

Remembering Ray's warning, I decline. Seth tries incessantly to persuade me to drink it, practically pouring it down my throat himself. But I stand my ground, and after a grueling few minutes of pressure, Ray rips the glass from Seth's hand, pours the poison down his own throat, and slams it on the table as if to say "ENOUGH!"

The way everyone looks around at each other confirms my fears. There was something in that glass meant for my lips only. Though I feel relieved to have avoided the toxin, I'm not sure Ray should have consumed it either, a fear later validated. I think he was feeling the same fear but, for whatever reason, he couldn't give a damn.

As we pass through the lobby, we are closely watched by the salivating wolves in the lobby. But I am still breathing, a feat that seems incredible at this point. The weekend's events have also stirred the warrior within me. I am more than surviving now; I am pissed off about the whole situation. Don't get me wrong. I still believed I could be *offed* at any moment, but the very fact I had subverted all attempts so far, accompanied with a growing intuition that I wasn't fighting this battle alone empowered me. Other than myself, I trusted only Ray, and that was with a cautious reserve. But I had me.

After we climb from the cab at the Armoury, I keep a generous arm's distance between me and every stranger I encounter. If my space is intruded upon, I immediately jockey into an opposing direction. Whether it is ebbing and flowing on the dance floor or standing on the sidelines, there will be no question for any observer what my intentions are. With the fear of death guiding me, I have decided to take no chances.

I am the first to pay and enter. No sooner than I have been admitted do Seth, Ray, and the others turn and walk away. When I move to follow, the gatekeeper tells me I won't be allowed back in if I leave. I am stuck. I have no idea where they have gone, and I am not about to get trapped alone on the dark street. My only option is to wait and hope they return.

I wander around inside, checking the place out, but remain within view of the entrance. The hostility around me feels heavy. There is no mistaking the anger in their faces. I am on high alert and guard my space fiercely. I still can't understand how so many strangers in such a large foreign city could be aware of what is happening, and why they are all pitted against me. After nearly an hour, my *friends* finally return. When I ask where they went, everyone just stares at me but says nothing.

Realizing they'll never tell me, I say, "Go to hell."

Once inside, they quickly disburse into the sea of dancing, sweaty bodies. I attempt to stay close to Ray, but he seems distracted now, so I return to my protective party of one. Seth keeps pulling up to me and cursing me in my ear, saying I am a terrible boyfriend and an untrustworthy friend. I try to argue the obviousness of my case and question how my trying to save my own ass makes me a bad person, but in typical Seth-style when he is high on meth, reasoning and common sense fall on deaf ears. It seems like he is trying to give the impression that he isn't with me but, rather, against me. I wondered if he was making this distinction out of fear for his own safety or if he truly hated the fact that I was still alive.

After a few hours of doing my best to enjoy the music and light show, dancing around like a paranoid boxer, I begin to feel some relief. The sun begins to rise and with no apparent attempts on my life, I wonder if maybe I am out of danger now. I call Jan and let her know I am okay. I then call Jeff and leave a message detailing briefly what happened and let him know that I am okay. Finally I call Benjamin and do the same.

As the party begins to wind down, we collect ourselves and return to the hotel. When we arrive, Seth and his gang go inside, but Ray and I hold back. He suggests we go for a walk to McDonald's, a few blocks away. I think he is really trying to keep me out of the hotel for some unknown reason. When we return, he calls Seth, and after a quick conversation, he hangs up and says we shouldn't go up, that Seth still seems very wound up. Knowing these people, it is more likely that a group sex party is taking place, one that is sure to involve the "secret" that I am being punished for knowing. I don't push it though, feeling lucky to be alive.

After a while, Seth starts calling me, wanting to know where I am and why I haven't come to the room. I enjoy his frustration and don't offer much information to him. *Doesn't feel good, does it?*

He keeps calling, losing more of his confidence with each call. It's kind of fun; for once, I feel like the puppet master. Doubtful that I really have any control, I look up and around wondering if maybe Seth is watching us, but this side of the building has no windows and I don't see anyone on the streets. Ray finally says we should return to the room. Before we go up, he stops me and looks at me with a seriousness that I don't expect. Staring into my eyes, he says, "David, if there ever comes a time when I have to choose between my friendship with Seth or you, I will choose you. Don't forget that, okay?"

As sincere as this feels, I sense it isn't as sincere as he wants me to believe. I don't trust anybody at face value anymore. I nod, and we go inside.

Back in the room, everyone is lying around in sweats and shorts, winding down from whatever. Seth is now being overly loving and affectionate to me, acting like the man I fell in love with. So we lie down together and talk like two lovers without a problem in the world.

Oh love, my kryptonite. I didn't know how to protect myself from its use against me. Love was the great weapon in all of this, a weapon I was powerless against.

Kurt listens in and injects his bits of venom whenever he can. I knew he despised me, but Seth always pretended not to see it. At one point as we lie there, I tell Seth that I feel I have been touched by an angel.

Kurt spews, "You weren't touched by an angel. You got fucked by the devil."

"Kurt, shut the fuck up!" Seth replies.

Soon we are all packed up and ready to go. I pay the bill, and we hit the road. The line of cars crossing the Canadian border is very long, and it takes a couple of hours to get through. At one point Ray, Kurt, and I decide to step out and smoke under a tree. I tell Seth to man the wheel as the line moves forward at a crawl. It feels good to leave him behind. While the three of us sit in the grass smoking, I look back at Seth. He is angry, pounding the steering wheel with his fist, probably frustrated with the way things turned out. I can tell it is a moment he thinks is private because of the startled look that washes over his face when he catches my stare.

Back in Seattle, we arrive at Seth's. Ray quickly leaves and Seth asks me to take Kurt home. I resist, but Seth begs me, so I do it. On the way, the way Kurt keeps staring at me makes me uncomfortable. He begins to quietly speak. It sounds like a funeral eulogy, "Dearly beloved, we are gathered here to say goodbye to this soul …" This goes on until we arrive at his apartment.

Before he steps out, he thanks me for my generosity and then says, "You know, David, I really do like you. You are a good person. But you realize you are going to die, don't you?"

With that, his gaze lingers, and then he climbs out, shuts the door, and walks away.

With Friends like This …

The next day, Benjamin came home and we talked about the trip. He didn't say much but looked really surprised when I shared the details. I asked him again what he meant about the clocks and I told him about the large clock and face on the stage. He didn't seem to know anything about it, but said we should go online to the chat rooms and see if anyone else knew anything. It didn't take very long to find people who had attended, but when we started asking questions, they wouldn't give any details about the events.

Finally one guy asked us to go private with him. He told us who the performer, a female impersonator, was and asked us not to say who had told us. Back in the public chat room, somebody started warning people about who I was and that they'd better not talk to me. In a matter of minutes, we emptied that chat room.

I then told Benjamin I knew something about all of this. I was going to tell him what I knew about the secret. He instantly had a sense of where I was going and begged me to tell him what I knew. The obsessive demands he started putting on me suddenly frightened me, and I decided I shouldn't talk about it. He became angry and started yelling at me, demanding I tell him what I knew. This freaked me out, so I told him to get out of my room, and I closed and locked the door. He then started pounding on the door, insisting that I tell him what I knew. I was shocked by how quickly he had shifted. It was like Dr. Jekyll and Mr. Hyde.

He then came back and told me he knew I was doing drugs in the house and was going to call the police and the landlord and have me evicted. I panicked and called Seth.

"David, I tried to tell you that you can't trust him. What are you going to do?"

"I don't know what to do. I don't want to be here."

"Why don't you come stay with me? I really miss you."

"Come on, Seth, you know I can't do that."

"Why?"

"Why? Have you forgotten about Canada?"

"David, it's over now. We were high and it got weird. I'm sorry. I promise you nothing will happen. You need to get away from there. It's not safe with him. Just come for a few days until you figure out what to do. I promise you'll be safe here."

After a short internal struggle, I decided to go. I packed some clothes, locked my bedroom door, and left.

Not long after we arrived home from Vancouver, Ray became really sick. He was running a fever well over 100° for several days. He became disoriented and increasingly worse. A couple days later, Seth called me distressed, saying Ray had called crying and babbling incoherently. He was somewhere in the neighborhood, so I drove to Seth's and we went out looking for him.

I found him a few blocks away, sitting in a parking lot. When I walked up to him, he was crying, covered in sweat, and drooling. He seemed confused and lost. At first he didn't recognize me, but I shook him and yelled his name until he did. Seth ran up and we carried him on our shoulders back to his place.

He had apparently gone to the emergency room, but he said they wouldn't help him. There was no doubt in my mind that his condition was the result of whatever was in that drink he had in Canada. Within a few days he recovered and the three of us never discussed it again.

A few days later, I decided to return home to my room with Benjamin.

Keep Moving

The following couple of weeks grew increasingly unbearable at home with Benjamin. With his cold treatment and continuing threats of police and eviction, it didn't take long for me to realize I had to move. Seth allowed me to stay with him until I could find a place. I looked at several apartments but wasn't finding anything I liked in my price range. With funds running low and my credit cards filling up, I had to really start watching my money, so I could no longer afford the new expensive places I was accustomed to.

Seth suggested that I move into his old building, just a few blocks off Broadway. He thought the manager, a fellow drug user, might give me a deal. At first I hesitated, but after finding nothing else, I checked into it. I had heard the stories about the place. I knew Jess, the manager, was a seriously sketchy meth addict who had lots of sex parties. He creeped me out but gave me a lease on terms I could afford, so I ignored the red flags. I certainly didn't think enough about it to realize he was connected to this dark underworld I was caught up in.

The first sign of trouble came when Jess kept delaying my move-in. Benjamin was threatening to lock me out, so I finally had to move my belongings into the parking garage of the building, unprotected, because Jess wouldn't give me the keys. He said the re-carpeting was taking longer than he expected, but in truth I thought it was something much more sinister that was causing the delays. I wondered if wires were being dropped through the walls, just as they had been when I lived with Seth. There was no chance I would sit quietly through that again, so keeping me away until it was completed seemed an obvious solution. But I was out of money and options, so I just told myself it wasn't happening.

When I finally received the keys, I took a day off work so I could start moving. Seth, Ray, Ricky, and I spent the next three days nonstop painting and moving. Of course, Tina was there helping too. We didn't do anything without her anymore. And this weekend turned out to be another trip down the rabbit hole.

The "strange" element entered the scene almost immediately. Ricky was a super sketchy guy, and the higher he was, the weirder he got. Seth and Ray switched into a mindset similar to the one I'd experienced in Canada. As we worked, they held their private meetings, sometimes with Ricky too. I was always kept beyond listening distance. Oh, how I wish I hadn't been so passive in those situations. What else might I have learned if I had been more aggressive?

I suddenly feel foolish for having allowed all this to happen again. I had nearly escaped them, but like it or not, my life had become enmeshed with these people. And not much had changed. I was still hopelessly in love with Seth, and this was still the hook, line, and sinker for me. And now I was a drug addict, just like him. I played games with myself, assuring myself that I could handle it this time. I made myself believe that everything happening was my fault, and if I tried hard enough, with Seth's help, it would all be okay. It's strange how quickly I was assimilated into something that would have seemed impossible before then. This was all somehow becoming normal to me. I'd been immersed in it so long that I was forgetting what life was like before I met him.

While working in the kitchen, painting and cleaning, I start noticing Ricky's strange behavior. He keeps making secret rooms behind furniture the way a child would build forts. Inside, he is coloring pictures on the backs of pages of poems with colored pencils. But it is what his body is doing that catches my attention. He is displaying that tell-tale behavior of the secret, but in a different way from what I'd witnessed so far. It is as though he is short-circuiting because every minute or so, he jerks around as though a current of electricity is flowing through him. I can tell it is frustrating him, and the more it happens, the deeper he tries to hide.

"Ricky, are you okay?" I ask.

"Yea, I'm fine," he says, clearly looking distressed and not fine. Just as he says this, his body jerks so hard he snaps his pencil in half.

"Ricky, what is wrong with you?"

Ray overhears us and tries to pull my attention away.

"He's just high, David. You know how he gets. Ricky, why don't you go back to my house? Richard is there."

"I don't want to. I'm okay. I'll go up on the roof for a while." He gathers up his poems and pencils, puts everything into a small box, and heads out the door. Just before he leaves, he looks back at me with desperate eyes.

"Ricky, go!" Ray says.

My apartment was like living in a fishbowl. The apartment buildings adjacent to mine had full view into every room but my bathroom. There were no window coverings yet, so we had to hang sheets to create whatever privacy we could. I suddenly noticed a man on a balcony across from mine staring in, watching us. Now I understood why Ricky was hiding behind the furniture. Anytime I went to the window or out on the balcony, there he'd be, smoking a cigarette and watching.

With Ricky gone, we continue painting and unpacking. After a few hours, Seth and Ray grow concerned with Ricky's whereabouts, so I say I'll go check on him. When I get to the roof, I find him sitting at a picnic table coloring. I sit across from him and watch. It is so strange what is happening to him. He seems like he is experiencing that pleasure I'd come to recognize in the others, but there continues that periodic jolt of electricity that obviously causes him pain. I start asking vague and disguised questions about the secret, thinking maybe he will tell me something. He then pushes over a pile of his poems and says I should read them. As I do, I realize they are about the secret, but not anything you could detect unless you already knew something about it.

I am stunned. Never have I gotten such a direct confirmation of what I knew existed, what those in my circle always denied.

I tell him I wish that I could be part of "the club."

He looks up at me and says, "Don't worry, honey, you will."

I smile and keep reading.

Ricky was a very interesting character. He had quietly taken it upon himself throughout this entire time to collect poems of seemingly relevant subject matter from famous poets and email them to the group. If he wasn't emailing them, he was writing them out and coloring pictures on the back. He spent many hours at the library compiling these poems. I guess he'd been doing this long before I arrived, but he added me to the list of recipients and I started receiving the emails as well. Sometimes we'd start up a private correspondence. It was during some of these that he told me a little about his history. He said he had grown up being taught about the esoteric Gnostic teachings of Christianity. He said that that knowledge was very much at play in our lives today. He never told me much more than that, but he assured me that one day I'd understand everything. As I learned this, he no longer seemed so sketchy and lost to me.

Without warning, Seth and Ray appear on the rooftop, startling us with their arrival.

"What are you doing?" Ray yells at Ricky.

"Nothing, I swear. We're just talking. Aren't we, David?"

"Yea, we're just talking and I'm reading his poems."

They are suspicious, even alarmed. Ray grabs a handful of the poems and starts reading through them. He then looks up at Seth and shakes his head.

"Ricky, pack your shit up. You need to leave," Ray says.

"Why, I didn't do anything. We're just talking."

"What did you say to him? You must have said something?" Seth demands.

"Let's go back to the apartment." Ray says. He grabs the rest of Ricky's things, pulls him by the arm, and pushes him toward the stairwell.

Shocked by what's happening, I quietly follow.

Back in the apartment, Ray and Ricky talk heatedly about something in the living room. I hold back and watch from the hallway, out of sight of anyone beyond the windows. Ray is mad and Ricky is frightened, defending himself.

"I didn't say anything. We were just talking," he says.

"Well, you must have said something," Ray yells.

"I swear I didn't do anything," Ricky cries back.

By now, Ricky is practically convulsing. With each electrical jolt that fires through his body, he spasms and finally drops to the floor. He tries to ignore it, but with each spasm, he becomes more distressed.

Ray's phone rings. He answers and responds, "Yes, he knows. I don't know." Then he starts pacing around explaining that he isn't sure, like he and the caller are trying to figure something out. When he looks at Seth, I can see that Ray is panicked. Then Ray looks at Ricky and says, "Your poems. Where are your poems?"

"Here, in this box. Why? It's nothing, just dumb poems and drawings," Ricky says.

Ray pulls them out, scattering them on the floor. He talks for a few more minutes and then hangs up. He tells Ricky to put everything in the box. Then he looks at me and asks about the paint we are using.

"What are you talking about?" I ask.

"The paint. Is it latex?" he yells.

"I don't know what kind of paint it is! What the hell is wrong with you?"

He rushes over to a can, picks it up, and starts reading the label.

The paint was part of the Ralph Lauren "Suede" collection. They were very dark colors that had a sand-like synthetic additive. When they dried, it looked as though you had wallpapered with suede. It was beautiful stuff. Because of its nature, we were putting on several coats trying to achieve an even texture.

"It's not latex, David. Did you ask Jess if you could paint?" Ray is insistent.

Before I answer, his phone rings again. He explains what he knows about the paint. He grows increasingly agitated and after he hangs up, he walks up to one of the walls we are painting, forcefully presses his thumbs into what appears to be two purposeful spots, and twists them to rub the paint away. He looks at us with a frustrated look and again asks, "Did you ask Jess if you could paint?"

"No!" I reply. "What's the big deal? When I move, I'll paint it white."

"Jess is pissed that we are painting. You need to go downstairs and talk to him."

"It's 3 in the morning, Ray! How does he know we're painting?"

"Just go!" I look at Seth and he nods in agreement.

"This is fucking crazy," I say as I walk out the door.

I take the elevator down to the courtyard and find Jess gardening on his patio. Through the windows I see there are several people milling about in his living room. He seems to want to keep my attention from them by positioning himself so that I have to turn my back on them to see him.

"Why didn't you tell me you were painting?"

"I didn't think it was a big deal."

"It's not latex paint."

"So what? It's indoor paint, Jess. I don't know why you are so upset."

"You really should have told me you were going to paint."

"Well, I'm sorry. I really didn't think it was such a big deal." I look back at the people in his apartment and then back at him.

He follows my eyes. "I really wish you would have asked."

"I said I'm sorry. I'll paint it white before I move." I turn and walk away.

When I get back to my apartment, Seth and Ray are talking and Ricky is under my bed trembling uncontrollably. I can't keep my eyes off of him. Finally, Ray tells Ricky to pack his things up and go back to his apartment a few blocks away.

"Why? I don't want to leave, Ray."

"Just go!"

"Do I have to give them my poems?" he asks.

Seth and Ray both yell at him to shut up and leave. He gathers his things and hesitantly makes his way to the door. I notice the frightened look in his eyes as he is forced out. A few hours later he returns, crying hysterically. He is at the locked gate, but they won't buzz him in. After a long, dramatic pleading, he leaves. (The following week, Jess told me that Ricky was banned from the building. When I asked why, he cut me off and walked away.)

Things calm down and Seth invites us into the kitchen to have some more Tina. We sit on the floor at Ray's request, I assume to hide us from the view of the windows and the man who keeps watching us. Seth leaves to go to the bathroom.

"David," Ray says, "you need to be careful and watch what you say. You could get us in a lot of trouble, and we might not always be around to protect you."

After everything that has just happened, I'm too afraid to say anything. I just nod.

The rest of the weekend is quiet but sketchy. Ray and Seth are both suffering the same painful jolts and spasms that Ricky was experiencing. My fear grows as I watch them jerk and wince in pain. All the while they continue painting and carrying on like nothing abnormal is happening. After what Ray had said, I become fearful of saying anything, so I just try to ignore everything and work. From time to time, emotion overcomes me and I have to fight hard to hold the tears back, sometimes fleeing to the bathroom to regain my composure. I know the closed door of my bathroom provides me little if any privacy; it is just a desperate attempt to pull myself together.

We continue to paint and unpack. Every few hours, we stop to do more Tina. I begin to think about the drugs we are doing. I realize how much our use has gone beyond clubbing now. We are getting high just to get high. I also realize my relationship with Seth revolves around heavy drug use. This is the first time I admit to myself that my drug use is no longer recreational. It feels dirty, and so do I.

Sunday morning, Seth starts talking about going to Everett that afternoon for dinner with his family. This comes out of nowhere and I can't believe that he wants us to spend time with his family after having been up without sleep for four days. We are a mess!

He says we have to go and tells Ray we may have to stay there overnight depending on how things play out. He looks worried. I sense this is somehow related to what happened with Ricky and Jess.

"Seth, I can't be around your family like this. I am way too sketchy. There's no way I can do it."

"You'll be fine, David. We don't have a choice. We have to go."

"Why didn't you tell me this earlier? I would have stopped getting high."

"I forgot about it until now." He looks to Ray for help. I know something is wrong, but I know he won't tell me what.

A few hours later, we shower and head out the door. Ray stays behind, continuing to work. On the way there, we stop by Home Depot to pick up another can of paint. Our priorities aren't making much sense now, but I keep quiet and let Seth lead the way. I can't get my mind off of where we are going.

In Home Depot, things become very strange, reminding me of our time in Canada. He holds my hand and pulls me through the store at a fevered pace. Many of the other people in the store have that same angry aggressive attitude toward us, just like Canada. There is panic happening in every direction, like cockroaches scattering from light. Seth is careful to keep us in the view and company of employees. As we wait for our paint to be mixed, we sit and I watch in amazement the fervor with which people are running around and watching us, discussing us to each other and on cell phones. It's like they are in damage control. I tell myself I'm being paranoid, but when I try to dismiss it as an affect of being high, nothing changes. Deep down, I know what I'm seeing is real and bizarre as hell.

Seth looks excited by all of the commotion. He also seems to fully understand what is a complete mystery to me.

With paint in hand, we walk out the door. An employee runs up behind us and strategically escorts us the full distance to the car, but without making it plainly obvious that he is doing so. All of it is so impossibly strange, yet exciting on some level. It feels like I am playing a main role in some mysterious performance known to everyone but me. We jump in the car and roar away.

Heading north on I-5 is no less sketchy. Seth maneuvers through the traffic like Mario Andretti. Vehicles are racing around us and upon us like hell's racers. As they fly past, I see the excited faces of drivers talking on their cell phones and frantically looking in their mirrors and dodging traffic like deranged commuters late for work, all the while keeping an eye on us. They have the same "look" as those I'd witnessed in Canada.

I become so frightened that I recline my seat completely, fearing that someone might try to shoot at my head. A glance over to Seth reveals his excitement to everything happening. He is loving every minute of this.

We finally arrive at our safe house in Everett. It is the home of his uncle, a big expensive house, probably 100 years old. We are invited to a small room at the back of the house. After we go through the formalities, Seth, his dad, and his uncle excuse themselves. I sit on the love seat alone for what seems like a very long time, wondering where I am, who these people are, what their intentions might be, what is going to happen next, and if I will make it out alive. Finally they return. Soon after, the wife brings us cans of unopened soda and everyone carries on like nothing is amiss. I am introduced to two young girls who quickly excuse themselves and then a young boy, probably 10 or so. He is wearing a white T-shirt with a silk-screened photo of him and another boy, his best friend, or so he says. Above the picture is the tagline "Party Animals." He tells me that it is a new shirt, made especially for this day. Then his parents ask him to perform for us. He bashfully, then eagerly, bursts into a performance of "Highway to Hell" by AC/DC, complete with air guitar and a dramatic knee-slide across the hardwood floor.

I can hear trains off in the distance, and for some curious reason, these trains worry me. Not too much after that the grandparents arrive. Everyone goes out back and gathers at the two picnic tables. The adults sit at one, and Seth and I sit with the kids at the other. As I sit there gripped in fear, I look around into the other yards, through the fence slats, up at the other windows, searching for a sniper or some other hidden surprise that could turn the cards on me.

Soon dinner is served and as everyone eats, I sit petrified, staring at my food, trying to figure out what all of this means. When I look up, I notice Seth's young niece, probably 12 or so, staring at him from across the table with a look of complete disgust and loathing. She is extremely angry with him, as though she detests what she is witnessing. With my ability to hold it together about to fail, I excuse myself and go to the bathroom. I hide in there as long as I can, pouring through the data trying to figure out where this is leading.

As I emerge from the bathroom, I look up the hallway to the front room, and I'm drawn to the porch beyond. I ignore the desire to do the right thing by rejoining everyone and instead walk through the house to the porch and sit on the steps. I look up and down the street, searching for anything out of the ordinary.

There is a sudden cool breeze. It feels nice, reminding me of sitting on my porch as a kid, watching the summer rain. I so wish I could be there right now.

Seth suddenly appears, snapping me out of my daydream, asking me why I haven't rejoined them. I say nothing; I just stare out at the sky.

Minutes later his dad comes out. Seth silently returns inside. His dad stands next to me and casually, with his hands on his hips and staring out in the same direction I am, asks me how I am doing.

"I'm fine," I reply, though I'm sure he can hear the lack of trust in my tone.

He looks down at me, smiles, and sarcastically says, "Sure you are." He then walks back inside.

Deciding I have had enough, I find Seth and tell him I am ready to go. I toss a quick goodbye to his dad, walk out the front door, and up the street to my car. Seth has my keys, so I pace the street looking for signs of trouble until he arrives.

Pretending confusion, he asks, "What's wrong?"

I just glare at him and say, "Nothing, Seth. Just take me home."

An Unexpected Friend

It's the second weekend of September, early Sunday morning, and we have just returned to my apartment after leaving the club. I notice Seth paying an unusual amount of attention to some guy on the street as we are making our way into the apartment complex. It is obvious that something strange is going on, but I observe and say nothing.

In my apartment, Seth suddenly says that he forgot something and needs to run home to get it. Knowing exactly what is happening, I stare into his eyes, attempting to reveal my disgust with his lie. He registers my suspicion but goes anyway.

As I watch him from my balcony, I see the other guy follow in his path, so I decide to give pursuit. I slip through the security gate, sneak up the street, and as I round the corner, I hear someone calling my name. I freeze in my tracks and look around.

Diagonally across the street is a boy I know from the clubs, Jake. This throws me off; I can't make sense of it. It is 7 in the morning, and there is nobody on the streets except for him and me. I look down the street just in time to see Seth turning off with the other guy following. I look back at Jake, who is now crossing toward me. He seems also to be watching Seth's progress as he starts to talk to me.

I make it obvious that I am distracted, but he positions himself in front of me, studies his surroundings, and pulls me into an inescapable session of small talk. As I respond to his questions, I attempt in vain to continue my pursuit. He seems sincere when he asks me if I am okay. It catches me by surprise, the genuine look of concern in his eyes.

"No, I'm not doing okay." Giving up my pursuit of Seth, I tell him what I am doing, and how crazy everything has become. I don't know him very well, but in the few things he says to me, I know immediately that he is completely aware of what I am going through.

"David, I can't believe that you and I haven't become friends by now. You would really like my friends."

"How can you say that? You don't even know me."

113

"I know you better than you think. I know you need help. We've been through this; we understand what's happening to you."

Completely surprised, I give up pursuing Seth and turn my attention solely to Jake, who goes on talking.

"There is another way to deal with this craziness, David, but you need to get away from the drugs and those people you are hanging around with. That's going to end badly for you if you don't."

"I don't know how to, Jake. I don't know anybody else. And they won't let go of me."

"You should come to one of our meetings. We have coffee every Sunday at Starbucks, up on Broadway."

"You mean a support group, like AA?"

"No, it's just me and my friends. You'll like it, I promise. We can talk about what's happening to you, help you understand. Why don't you take my number and think about it? If you decide you want to come, call me."

I pull out my cell phone and enter his digits. He then takes a good look around and seems to come to some private satisfaction with what he takes in. He says goodbye and disappears back in the direction he'd come from. Realizing it has been too long to catch Seth at anything, I continue around the block and double back to my place.

When I enter my apartment, I am surprised to find Seth sitting at my computer. He is logged into the chat room we met through. He attempts to hide what he is doing, but because he is unfamiliar with the Mac OS, I quickly understand what he is attempting to hide.

"Get the hell out of my house!"

"David, you need to calm down. It's not what you think."

"Yes, it is, Seth. Get out. Now!"

"Where have *you* been?" he says, trying to turn the cards on me.

"Looking for you! I watched that guy follow you to your house, Seth. I'm not a fucking idiot. Now get out!" I push him out the door, slam it behind him, and lock it. I turn immediately to my computer to look more closely at whomever he was chatting with.

To my surprise, he was chatting with himself. After a few minutes of bewildered investigating, I understand what was going on. The guy who had followed him home was likely still at his apartment, logged into his account, and he was chatting with him, on my computer, in my house. I had finally caught him in a lie. It had only taken a year to do, but I finally caught him. He was using my computer to hook up with someone else, and I caught him. I thought briefly about following him home and killing him and his date. Thank God I didn't.

My New Roommate

My relationship with Seth quickly deteriorated after that weekend. With the undeniable evidence I had, evidence I could finally hold onto and believe, I was able to begin convincing myself that he was the dishonest, dangerous man I suspected him to be. Until then, I could never let go of my love for him in order to get away from him. The illusion of who I thought he was when I met him, my insecurity that allowed him to control and manipulate me, his life of drugs that had now become mine, all of it combined to overpower my ability to think clearly and protect myself. Until now. Finally, it seemed I had started to tire of his manipulation, tired of searching in vain for answers about his secret, and tired of being the other man, playing second fiddle to his love and devotion of that secret.

More times than not I'd call him to find he was "in the bathtub," the place he always was if he wasn't at work or with me. And with that came the typical disorientation, heavy breathing, and strange behavior that I'd come to know so well. He now seemed addicted to this thing because every moment he was away from work and away from me, he was under its spell. And I had grown tired of all of it.

During this time of separating from Seth, Ray moved himself to center stage in my life. He worked hard to help me finish putting my apartment together and counseled me on surviving my dying love for Seth. Day after day while I struggled under the debilitating depression of my broken heart, he was there, painting, unpacking, and taking care to polish my little urban box into a beautiful home. I'll never forget the day when I walked through my front door and down the hall, feeling miserably depressed by my life, when my eyes fell upon this gorgeous place. I recognized everything as mine, plus a few things he had picked up from the VV (gay code for the Value Village thrift store). I couldn't believe how wonderfully he had understood my taste and how carefully he'd turned this fishbowl of an apartment into a warm beautiful expression of me. Tears ran down my face as I took it all in and thanked him for such a wonderful gift. In light of all that had happened in Canada and all that he had been doing for me over the past weeks, I began to trust him.

As Ray was taking control of my world, he was losing control of the one he shared with Richard, who wasn't working or paying his portion of the bills. He was also lying to the landlord, and to Ray, about the situation. This eventually blew up and they lost the apartment. Richard moved away, and Ray asked if he could stay with me until he found other arrangements. Considering all he had done for me, I happily offered my place to him.

One late evening, we were on the balcony smoking and talking about whatever unimportant subjects would distract my mind from the elephant in the middle of the room. I was still feeling pretty frustrated with Seth and everything else. As we sat there talking, I realized "the smoking man" was sitting on his balcony watching us again. I had had it with him. I started to yell at him, to ask him what the hell he was staring at, but before I could get much out, Ray grabbed me by the shoulders and whispered into my ear, "Don't say anything. Just ignore him. Trust me, you don't want to mess with that."

"Why not, Ray? I'm sick of all of this shit. I'm tired, Ray. Take me out or let me go!" Angry, I went off on a rampage about this, that, and anything else I was pissed about, like a laundry list. I even mentioned the meth-crazed, sex-obsessed gay boys who roamed the streets all night long, searching for each other using the secret internal homing beacons that I knew was at the core of the "secret."

Astonished, Ray stared at me for a while and then said, "My God, you really have figured it all out. You know everything."

And that revelation left me speechless.

During the next week, things got crazy again. Seth and I began to talk. It was just on the phone, a distance I decided was safe for me. Because he and Ray were friends, it was hard to keep him completely out of my life.

That Friday, I caught him in another lie that sent me over the edge. He said he was meeting friends after work for beers, something Seth would never do, mostly because he had a strong judgment against consumers of alcohol. Talk about the pot calling the kettle black. I figured out that he was really meeting up with some guy he met online.

I exploded! I packed up everything I still had of his into garbage bags, wrote a nasty letter, marched down the street to his apartment, and dumped the bags on his doorstep. I then called him back and left a blistering goodbye. After all I'd been through, all we'd been through, it was too much.

After dropping off the bags at his door, I went directly to see Ray where he worked and vented my anger onto him. He gave me the old "tsk, tsk, I told you so," so I stomped off in a dramatic huff back to my apartment. It was another very painful moment in a growing list of painful moments.

Seth later apologized for his dishonesty, which did little but add to the already foolishly long list of why I was an idiot to still be sitting on this ride.

And why was I still on that ride? There's no easy answer. Seth was a master manipulator, for sure. He had me dancing around like a marionette. My life had never come so intimately into contact with anyone like him before, and I was totally unprepared for what he put me through.

It sounds hokey to say, but I had an innocence before I met him, one that prevented me from seeing, or believing, who he was. And I was deeply in love with him despite it all. I feel now like I understand and can relate to anyone who has stayed too long in an abusive relationship. I was perfect for it when we met. Unhappy, lonely, suffering from a damaged self image and social anxiety, I longed to be popular, I needed to be in love. My long list of insecurities made me ripe for his manipulation.

And this secret I was chasing had me caught like a deer in headlights. I was hypnotized by it. The pleasure it brought to those who experienced it, I had to know what it was. The mystery of why it was so secret, and why I was forbidden to know, drove me crazy. And then there were the drugs and the club scene. It was some of the most exciting fun I'd ever had with my body. Ask Britney, Paris, Lindsay, or anyone else who's been there. This was literally the highest, most exciting time of my life and it was the most destructive, dreadful time, all rolled up into one.

After talking to Ray, I returned home and sulked, my heart ripped to pieces again. In a strange coincidence, I received an email from a guy I had been attracted to since before I'd known Seth. Andy and I met in the same chat room that Seth and I had, but we never got beyond a few conversations. In light of everything, I called him. Turnabout was fair play, right? No it isn't. It just makes everything worse. The mistake of tit for tat is a hard lesson I learned during this chapter of my life. When I look back, the idea that I allowed the behavior of anyone to give me permission to sacrifice the principles that govern who I am is one of my greatest regrets. These were a handful of ugly decisions that I wear upon my wounded soul like battle scars.

It turned out that Andy was in my building at that very moment.

Andy says he is visiting a friend in the building. He asks if he can stop by to say hi. I say sure, give him my unit number, and hang up. Before long, he is knocking on my door. I invite him in and we talk, getting to know each other. I hadn't planned on anything happening, but he starts rubbing my leg as he shares with me how long he has wished for this day to happen. He is very sexy, and I too had fantasized about this moment. It seemed whenever Seth and I were on the splits, like magic, Andy would pop onto my radar, almost as if he somehow knew. This was the first time it had ever gone beyond Internet chat though.

Right in the middle of our encounter, Ray walks in, and he is pissed. I had left a hastily written note on the door, telling him I was entertaining, but he ignored it. I step out of the bedroom, at his request, and follow him to the kitchen. He just stares at me, stunned.

He cries out, "David, why? Don't you see what they are trying to do?

"They? Ray, what are you talking about?" I pretend to not understand that something larger than an encounter is happening, in hopes that I can gleam some truth. I hated not understanding that something bigger was happening to me without my consent. I was always hoping for that someone to look me in the eye and reveal the truth to me because they knew I deserved to know everything that was happening to me.

Without answering me, Ray leaves. With the mood clearly spoiled, I ask Andy to leave. He understands and he too leaves. Then I begin to wonder. If Ray is right, if "they" are trying to do something to me, why would Andy leave so easily? It doesn't make sense.

I already had many signs that Ray was hoping that more was happening between us than friendship. Every time he looked me in the eyes and told me he loved me, followed by a long deep embrace, I was reminded that this was going in the wrong direction. But this had happened many times during my life and the mere act of pretending I didn't notice it had mostly prevented awkward situations from developing. Not so this time.

A few hours later he returns, very intoxicated. I can tell he had had a visit with Tina and probably a long visit with Gina. Teetering on the edge, he bursts through the door and begins his broken-hearted tirade. I run over to him to smooth things over and realize he's about to fall out.

At first he just looks at me and keeps telling me how much he loves me. I tell him I love him too, something I always do, but the way a sister tells a sister she loves her. He's despondent and teary-eyed. Then suddenly, he rips my pants down and attempts to move things forward. After a bit of a struggle, I pull my pants up and yell, "Ray, stop it!"

As happens on G, his mood turns dramatically. In a fit of anger, he pushes me away and curses me. But he is so close to the edge of falling out that he loses the thought as quickly as it had come. He starts stumbling and mumbling, so I change course and come to his aid. I ease him into my bed, and after a brief struggle, he passes out cold.

Knowing the pain of my shattered heart so well, I suddenly feel terrible as I watch him struggle in the grip of a G-hole. Like a broken-hearted lover turning to liquor to deal with rejection, I am witnessing the 21st-century gay version of such tragedy. I begin undressing him, first taking his shoes off, then his pants, and finally his jacket and shirt. As I am about to pull the covers over his body, I notice a strange movement within his abdomen. Ray is a skinny boy. I doubt there is an ounce of fat on his entire body.

Just above his right hip, I see a back-and-forth movement under the skin. It catches me off guard, stopping me in my tracks. I watch in disbelief. With him out cold, there is nothing now to prevent me from investigating this truth I have been pursuing so desperately.

My mind quickly plays through the guilt this situation presents. It doesn't take much to convince me I have to continue. I slowly place my hands upon his abdomen. A wave of energy washes over me as I hold them there, getting to know this elusive stranger.

It feels unnatural, the way it moves back and forth. It seems as though it is within the digestive tract. Probably something swallowed? Is it permanent or just an event limited by the journey from mouth to anus? Has it been implanted? I don't know. The rhythm is certain. Its movement is in step with the beating of his heart. I wonder if maybe this is natural to humans, so I use my body to verify it. I place my hands upon the same area of my body. Nothing. Maybe it's my position. I quickly lie down on the floor and check again. Nothing. I get back up and press against his abdomen again. There is definitely something in there.

I nudge him to see if he is truly out. Nothing awakens him, so I focus back on the strange movement. I use my fingers to explore the rest of his torso. Up, down, and all around. Having been subject to complete physicals continually since testing positive for HIV, I had become very familiar with the way a doctor looks for trouble within the torso. Everything brings me back to the strange movement. I hold one hand over his heart and the other over *it*. They definitely move in rhythm together. After nearly an hour of exploring and pondering, I realize that without slicing him open, there is nothing more I can do, so I give up.

I'm Losing My Way

The rest of the week was relatively normal, if normal includes coming home each day to find that your houseguest has rearranged the furniture *again* and snooped through every box and pocket you own during the process.

I wanted to believe Ray was just tweaked, but I was sure he was trying to keep a watchful eye on everything about me. I started leaving bait hidden around just to see if he'd find them. He did. Once he even figured out the combination to my safe and snooped around in there. I had no privacy with Ray in my house. I had a live-in mole watching my every move.

That Friday, John, a dealer and a friend of Ray's, dropped by. I guess he was a "friend" to me too, but I have since learned how to recognize a true friend. I didn't really have any friends during that time. Though my history with John predated Seth, we never really had taken the time to get to know each other. He was close to Ray, so that was probably why we ended up together that evening.

We sat and gossiped like big old queens. Two betrayed lovers, sharing in the pain of our hurtful men. He had actually survived an attempt on his life by his lover. While soaking in the tub, his boyfriend had apparently thrown a hairdryer into the bathtub. How he survived this was curious, but I had been through some very strange events, so who was I to judge?

So we shared our painful dramas. "Oh gurl, and do you know what he did next?" Blah, blah, blah. It was all strangely bonding. His candid discussion made me feel like he would be someone who could finally answer some of my elusive questions. He was a true player in this scene, and drugs were his cup of tea. And because I was still not ready to let go of the scene, I was happy to bring out the china. He pulled out a lot of Tina, and we proceeded to get really high. I had never done that much Tina in one sitting, ever. I'm lucky my heart didn't explode. I was ready to re-roof the entire building by the time we were done. With the both of us ready for lift off, he suggested we go downtown and do a "bit of shopping." We were in the car before the word "yes" fell from my lips.

I then remembered the tentative plans I had made with Jake and his boyfriend to see a movie that night. We were going to see *The Underworld*. He said it was well suited to what was happening in my life, so part of me was very curious to know what he wanted to share with me. But I never got the chance. Being high, I knew I wouldn't feel comfortable around them, so I cancelled.

My shopping expedition with John was insane. We whipped through the men's department of Nordstrom faster than *Queer Eye*'s Fab Five pouncing onto some tragic hetero for a makeover. It would be impossible to describe the sketchiness without a video, but when we walked out, the retail clerks were speechless. At one point, when one was asking me which pair of shoes I liked, I suddenly engaged in a two-way conversation with myself, an impromptu act of silliness that both John and I had been entertaining ourselves with all night. In turbo meth speed, I looked at one shoe and then at the other. Then I looked over my left shoulder and asked myself, "Which one do you like?" Without skipping a heartbeat, I looked over my other shoulder and *another* me responded in a frightening voice, "Which one, which one? Get them both, get them both." Think Smeagol in *Lord of the Rings*, in that schizophrenic smoker's voice of his. It was hysterical! I think the clerk wanted to run away in terror. Instead she stepped back and looked at me with an expression of "HELP, I have no idea what I'm supposed to do now."

After we left Nordstrom, things became very strange. While hunting for my car in the underground parking garage, both of us sensed something eerie lurking with us deep under the city. Looking to each other as we searched for my car, it was clear that we were both very spooked. When we finally found it, we quickly jumped in and bee-lined to the exit.

From there, we headed to deliver his "product" to a friend of his. I was basically along for the ride, only I was driving. She happened to live in the same building where Seth and I had had our short stint. She was a beautiful Italian girl, and she lived on the same floor that we had. She met us in the lobby.

As we walked down the hall to her unit, John introduced me. She stopped in her tracks, turned and looked at me, and said, "So, this is David."

Not really knowing what else to say, I responded with "The one and only." She seemed pleased to meet me, then returned to whatever had been consuming her thoughts before the introduction. She seemed to have a lot on her mind. In her apartment, she talked about her parents turning their backs on her for pursuing a life in the seedy underworld of techno clubs as a DJ. Her apartment was filled with DJ equipment. Though she was in her mid-20s, her wealth seemed obvious. I wished later that I had thought to investigate that equipment more than I did, as I'm sure it would have provided valuable information.

After they did their business, we all left together. Outside, she jumped into her black Porsche; we hopped into my black 350Z and drove off in different directions. Up the street, we pulled to a stoplight. Just as I was noticing the license plate of the car in front of me, 666-DYE, John's phone rang. He made motions to answer but said they hung up before he answered. He looked confused, handing me his phone, and pointing out the number of his caller. It was 666-6666. John seemed genuinely surprised by what had happened. I don't know if he was being honest, but I knew that that car in front of us and those plates were beyond his control. At that moment my fear factor tripped, my monster stirred to life, and I realized this was going to be a strange night.

We decided to go back to my place. John begged me to go out clubbing with him. He said it would be a great night for me if I did. I was high, I loved to go dancing, and it was an easy sale. As we headed out, he said he needed to make a few deliveries before the night's festivities. I offered to do the driving and he happily accepted.

The first stops were uneventful. I remained in the car as he ran inside to do business. On the third stop, something unexplainable happened. It was dark and I was parked on the street, waiting. A hundred feet or so in front and on the opposite side of the street, I noticed a dark figure leaning over the bed of a truck looking at me. A streetlight shone from above, filtering through a canopy of trees. His head was kind of bobbing up and down ever so slightly, almost cartoon-like, like some guy leaning over his truck, checking things out while trying to remain "cool." His face was in shadow but I could just make out his features: he was smiling. The strange thing about it was he didn't seem human.

I kept rubbing my eyes and stretching my head forward, attempting to get a better view. I remember thinking, "David, there is no way you are seeing what you think you are seeing." He looked like a creature from another world. I knew it was truly impossible for this figure to be standing there in front of me.

Suddenly, John opened the door and got into the passenger seat, and I nearly jumped out of my seat. Surprised, John asked what was wrong. I looked in the direction of what I had seen, but the stranger was gone. I turned back to John and he too looked in that direction and then back at me and flashed a devious smile and asked me what was the matter. I said it was nothing, nervously shifted the car into drive, and pulled away from the curb. As we drove quickly down the road, I looked back and saw that same figure again, watching us drive away. I looked at John, who was still smiling at me. I said nothing.

This event and that image has haunted me ever since. I wish I had had the courage to get out of my car and investigate, to know for certain what it was that I saw. Recently, I watched a preview for the movie *The Da Vinci Code*. My jaw hit the floor when right there on the screen I realized I was looking at the same face. It was the face of a gargoyle, one of many stone faces within the Temple Church of the Knights Templar in London. I can't know for sure what I saw that night, but I do know it was the same face upon the wall in the Temple Church.

Our next stop took us to within a block of Seth's apartment. Our destination happened to also be in the building of one of Seth's associates. It was an old brick four-story building with a rooftop addition. I've noticed many of these rooftop additions in urban neighborhoods. They look like shacks built atop the building. Seth had given me an in-depth history of his association with this man and his partner, in the same way he did with so much of his world that he introduced me to during our relationship. It was like getting a personal who's who tour of Hollywood's important faces by someone within the inner circle. I know that my introductions and history lessons were meant to register in my mind and stay there, even if I didn't realize it at the time.

When we pulled up, John looked at me with a profound seriousness and warned, "This is going to get really sketchy. Stay with me, okay?"

Feeling nervous about going, but afraid to be alone, I agreed. We climbed out of the car, studied our surroundings, then quickly walked across the street and up the stairs, and arrived suddenly at a door. John rings the bell.

Though it was dark inside, I heard somebody approaching. My heart was racing as the door opened. A sturdy man with hard features stared back at us. He had that same look that I had encountered in Vancouver, that *sinister* look. And he seemed very surprised to see me standing at his door. He then noticed John and hesitantly invited us in. He couldn't seem to take his eyes off me, and this made my fight-or-flight instinct ratchet up. He directed us to the living room, where we sat on the couch in front of the large bay window.

I looked out to the street and located my car, to get my bearings. I then looked back at John and realized the other guy was gone. A few moments later, he returned with another man. The other guy said hello to John but never took his eyes off of me. After a few moments of uncomfortably prying eyes, they pulled their attention away from me and engaged John in their business.

Once this was done, John said that we needed to get going. As we made our way to the door, one of the guys put his hand on my shoulder and invited me to stay and party with them. John grabbed my arm and said that we had other plans. I agreed and let him pull me out the door. As we stumbled down the steps, I looked back and saw both of them staring at me like they were watching a filet mignon walk off their plate. It was bone-chilling.

With all of our stops finally completed, and none too soon, we drove to the Cuff to party. We did a bit more Tina, popped a tab of Ellen, glanced in the mirror, and walked the half-block to the club.

Inside it was total madness. Packed wall to wall with boys dancing and playing, the music began to pour its deep thundering vibration into my spine, and with that, all sketch dissipated, replaced by the familiar environment of the clubs I enjoy so much.

Music and dancing has always been a great source of pleasure in my life. Since I came out many years ago, the gay club scene had become my musical playground, a place where I could escape the judgmental straight world and enjoy these pleasures in the safety of my tribe. Because of everything now happening in my life, this was changing. My tribe no longer felt so safe, my playground had become menacing, and even the music couldn't carry me away as it had before.

We slowly bounced our way through the crowded front bar, past the pool tables and dartboards, down the dark narrow stairway to the back where the dance floor was. The room was large and the ceiling high and the bass pounded through my chest. It was unusually packed. As we slipped our bodies through the sea of shirtless boys, something about what was happening started to frighten me. I noticed an unusual amount of attention from those around me, an eager, anticipating regard. My monster roared to life.

As we pushed through the crowd, many went out of their way to acknowledge me. This was strange because those days most of the attention I was receiving was negative. But that night, I was a celebrity again. The shift was clear as day and unnerving to me. I didn't trust it.

John stopped near the dance floor and struck a pose. Instantly boys pulled up and started talking to him. As usual, they drifted out of earshot as they conversed, all the while keeping tabs on my whereabouts. I stood by and bounced a little to the music, but mostly I scanned my surroundings, looking for any sign of trouble. Boys came up to me and smiled, said hi, patted me on the back, slapped my ass, and seemed eager. These were the same people who in the past had snickered behind my back and treated me with such disdain. I struggled to make sense of it.

I noticed that John was now distancing himself from me, standing off with the others. The way they looked at me while they talked, the way they smiled with that glint in their eyes, I sensed that something was wrong, that maybe I was not among friends. I began to feel I was in the dragon's lair. A boy I didn't know came up to me, grabbed my shoulders, looked at me face to face, and just smiled. I looked around and the people who were circling me were all looking at me and whispering to each other, just watching with that strange elation and whispering.

Suddenly, my inner alarm exploded into all-out fear. I knew something was happening and I didn't want to know what it was. Feeling overwhelmed, I snapped out of my frozen fear, walked up to John, and said, "I'm leaving."

Surprised and worried, he looked around for support in the faces of those around us and said, "Leaving! Why do you want to leave?"

"I'm not feeling well all of a sudden. I think I need to go home."

"Are you sure? The party is just starting."

"I'm not feeling well. I need to go."

"Do you want me to walk you to your car?"

"Yea, I do. Will you?"

"Yea, hold on." After talking to a few people, he and several of them escorted me to my car. "What's wrong?" he asked again.

"I don't know. Something feels wrong, and I don't like it."

They tried to talk me into staying, saying this was going to be a special night, but I couldn't shake the sense that I was in danger. I had to leave.

"Okay then. Let me give you something before you go," John said. He pulled out a small vial of liquid. I figured it was probably Gina. That was odd though. I had plenty of G that I had already purchased from him earlier.

"What is it?" I asked.

He looked smugly around at the others, and then back at me and said, "It's cyanide. You'll need it after tonight."

Not knowing what to think, I quickly studied the vial in my hand, then looked back at him, and feigned disregard. I jumped into my car and peeled rubber. I could literally feel darkness enveloping me as I drove away.

Feeling vulnerable, I decided to run to Jeff, the only person I trusted to protect me from impending danger. I pulled into an empty curb space around the block from his building and quickly ran down the street to the entrance, waving my security card over the electronic eye to gain entrance, and ran up the five flights of stairs to his apartment. Ever since Canada, I didn't trust elevators.

As I slipped into his apartment, he woke up startled and asked, "What's wrong?"

Obviously sketchy and frightened, I told him I had had a weird night and didn't want to be alone. Silently understanding, he hugged me and let out that worried mother exhale, and then put me to bed with him.

Hunting the Haunters

It was only a couple hours until he had to get up for work, and during that time, I regained a sense of security, though I was anxious to escape that bed. Tina and Ellen were working their way through my system, creating agony as I forced myself to lie motionless. With every twitch and movement, Jeff stirred in his sleep. To my relief, his alarm finally went off. He showered, slurped down a cup of coffee, and headed out the door, just as my foot hit the floor. I waited a bit and then left behind him. Back in my car, I drove the four blocks home. I quietly sneaked through the building and into my apartment, locked the door, and made my way to the couch. I sat in the dark until sunrise, slowly releasing the fear of the previous night's events. But I quickly realized that nothing could hide me or protect me from the invasive torture that my auditory system was falling victim to.

I guess you could call them auditory hallucinations, but I still don't exactly understand what was happening, though I have very strong theories.

It was always the same. The tormented voices I heard were people I knew. It started with Seth, and then gradually grew to include Ray, Dominic, Jeff, and ultimately members of my family. Faint voices traveling in on the air. Outside, they were louder. Inside, they were faint but everywhere. They grew louder when I brought my ear near a vent or air duct. I usually heard a constant horrifying screaming and pleading for it to stop, the sound of someone being tortured. "Please stop, please stop. No, no, oh my God, you're killing me. I hate you! I fucking hate you! You're killing me! Please, I don't want to die!" Mixed in with the pleading were the piercing terrified screams of someone in mortal pain. And I'll never forget the voice of the man who was inflicting the torture. I can still remember the images my mind created as I listened to him terrorize his victims. I could see his teeth gnashing and saliva spewing from his mouth as the pure evil roared from his mouth.

I deduced from what I heard that the pain was being inflicted by some kind of electric shock. After what I'd witnessed in Ricky, Ray, and Seth, I understood what was causing the agony, only this was much more intense.

One Sunday morning, after countless weeks of this, I decide to search for the source. Until now, I had been able to do little more than quietly endure the terror pouring in through my ears. On this day, driven by the need to bring silence to my mind, I could no longer just sit by helplessly.

Interestingly, the behavior of my two new cats provided a confirmation that this wasn't just craziness happening in my head. Whenever the attacks occurred, Sancho and Monkey began to behave strangely. They would cower close to me, following me wherever I went. They displayed the behavior of frightened animals, their ears and eyes responding to each drifting scream, nervously twitching to all the noises. I knew they could hear the terror that I was suffering under.

I had already concluded that it was coming from outside. Something I heard in the voices frightened me into thinking that the air in my apartment was dangerous, like it contained something poisonous or explosive. I rushed out onto my balcony for fresh air. I heard my niece's voice, and she was telling me to jump.

"Jump, David, you have to jump. They're coming for you. You have to jump." Not ready to believe what I was hearing, I stood motionless, listening. "Why won't he jump? You have to jump. It's the only way to escape."

I ran to my front door, thinking I would use the stairs instead. But when I looked out the peephole, I saw somebody standing at my door, a woman. I ran back out to the balcony.

"David, JUMP!" I heard.

Finally, I decided this was the only way out. So I climbed over the railing and lowered myself to the balcony below, and then to the next. When I was just one story above ground level, I tried to lower myself to a ledge, but I slipped and fell, smashing through a tree before crashing to the sidewalk below. I landed with a bone-jarring crash, my hip absorbing the energy of the fall.

With the intense pain that followed, I was sure my hip was broken. The pain nearly caused me to lose consciousness. Not wanting to be noticed by anyone, I forced myself up and tried to run away, but I was only able to drag my right leg. I gripped the wrought iron gate for several minutes and screamed silently as the pain poured through me. When I was finally able to regain my composure and stand on my foot, I realized that nothing was broken, though the basketball-sized bruise that was developing would take months to heal. After thanking God for helping me avoid tragedy, I returned to my quest. I set out on foot and slowly limped through the neighborhood, with the sound in my ears as my guide.

During this time, as my mental processing considered every possibility, I realized that it wasn't uncommon for someone under the spell of the drugs I had been doing to become paranoid and delusional. I'd watched family members battle addiction and the mental breakdowns it could bring. But I also knew my situation was different. There were too many hard facts, too many events out of my control, for me to accept insanity as the answer. I knew my drug-use wasn't helping, but I also knew that my mind wasn't the source of the events. It was merely reacting to them.

I thought about one of those events. One evening, while on Jeff's rooftop deck smoking a cigarette, I noticed a stranger who was up there for the same reason, watching me. I walked over to him and asked if he ever heard the screams of people being tortured drifting through the air in the neighborhood. He just looked at me and smiled a long smile, and then nodded his head and said, "All the time, kid." He wished me luck, smashed his cigarette out with his foot, and disappeared into the building, leaving me alone on that rooftop. I knew then as I know now that I was living through something very real and incredible.

I also believe that drugs and the mental breakdowns they can bring to those using them were probably the insurance my adversaries were counting on to protect themselves from me. Feeling helplessly outfoxed, I hovered on the edge of bringing it all to a tragic end for a very long time, but somehow I found the strength and help to keep going. Somehow, I don't doubt that forces beyond our world had a hand in that.

My search through the neighborhood took me that day to some surprising places. Initially I ended up at the Westminster Presbyterian Church, a large gothic chapel on the hill. The closer I got, the louder the screaming became. Just behind the church, there is a row of buildings that look like self-storage units, only built of brick in the same style as the church. I noticed the sign posted, warning me to keep out, but I continued anyway. When I wandered too far, a man came out of the church, looking around cautiously. Without coming too close to me, he asked me what I was doing. I could tell that my presence wasn't wanted so I apologized and left the same way I had come.

I walked around to the other side, onto a public parking lot that looked into the area I had just left. A tall chain-link fence protects that side of the property. Just beyond the fence is a sidewalk that leads down to a basement doorway. Spray-painted on the door in black were the words "KEEP OUT."

I stood at the fence for a while trying to zero in on where the sound was coming from. I was drawn back to that door. Several men came out of the church and watched me while they discussed something, then returned inside. Finally, the same guy who had questioned me earlier came up and asked, "Can I help you with something?"

"No, I'm fine."

"You need to move on."

"I'm on public property, I don't have to go anywhere."

Knowing he could do nothing, he left me alone, but he kept a watchful eye on me.

Ignoring him, I focused my listening on the storage buildings beyond. Maybe it was coming from there. I decided to walk around the block, hoping to find some other way that would get me closer. I passed the apartment building I had been in with John that strange evening not long before, and I realized the cries were much louder there. I looked around to make sure nobody was watching me and then I sneaked up to the side of the building, near a doorway. All the doors and windows on ground level were painted over and protected with security fencing, so it was impossible to look inside. I put my ear up to a window, and as soon as I did, I knew the screaming was coming from inside.

Startled, I stumbled backward and nearly fell over. I then positioned myself there for a while, listening, trying to figure out what was happening, the way a blind man attempts to understand what is going on in the world without the use of his eyes.

Eventually, the same two strangers from that night with John arrived. Because of the vintage car they were in, I realized they were the people Seth had once talked about. As they figured out who I was, I saw the alarm grow in their faces. It didn't take long for me to understand it was time to leave.

I continued around the block. I passed a gated path that led back to the building, but it was impossible for me to enter without bringing a lot of attention to myself. I continued down the street, heading home. As I passed a few other buildings along the way, I noticed that the screaming grew louder. I investigated as best I could, but because most everything was gated, I didn't get far. As I was walking through my courtyard, the cries grew louder when I passed a doorway of the building next door. It was a back entrance, locked and never used, probably an emergency exit. I had always suspected the sounds were coming from that building. I'd sit on my balcony day after agonizing day, staring at that building as I listened in terror.

Suddenly I realized a common denominator. I ran back out to the street and looked for the manholes. I followed them back to where I'd come from. As I got to each one, I bent down and put my ear close to listen. The sound was coming from underground, probably traveling through the maze of tunnels. That's why it was so hard to pinpoint, why it seemed to come from so many different directions.

Suddenly excited, I started talking myself into finding a way down there when a frightening realization stopped me. If there was something or someone down there, if I went down to investigate and got caught, no one would know where I was. There would be nothing to keep me from vanishing forever. Deciding the risk was too great, I returned home.

Who Is Going to Save Me?

The following weekend, Andy and I make plans to see a movie together. Ever since Jake's comment about *The Underworld*, I had really wanted to see it. During the movie, Andy asks, "If you had the choice of being a vampire or a Lycan (the name for the werewolves in the movie), which one would you choose?"

It seems a curious question, and not completely hypothetical. Intrigued, I play along. "I think I'd like to be a vampire, though both have their advantages." I suddenly hope this conversation will lead Andy to reveal the secret to me, initiating me into the society. The allure of their secret has me wanting to be one of them. The mysterious sexual pleasure I knew it could provide has cast a spell over me, a spell stronger than my fear of the pain I know it is also capable of. The more they try to hide it from me, the more I need to know.

I know Andy is just as much a part of it as Seth or Ray is, and I hope that he is going to give me what they won't. After watching the way he and Ray interacted in my apartment, and remembering that fateful night at the Mass event in Arena, when he was there, looking on with the rest of their cronies, as Seth paraded me around for their amusement, I know he is one of them.

Once, during sex, Andy had talked about wanting to keep me around, toying with me about my carcass being worth a couple million. The way he slipped it in, between moans, I might not even have noticed had I not been so well tuned to my sketchy environment. And well tuned also meant conditioned. This form of mind play had become a common occurrence in my life by then. What would otherwise be an obvious cue to run for your life had become just a normal element of mine, one crumb of the many clues I was collecting. Because of these and other revealing moments, I kept seeing Andy, in the hopes of discovering more about their world. And *of course*, part of me believed he really was falling in love with me, again my kryptonite.

After the movie, we return to my place to get ready to go out clubbing. There is a special event happening at Club Nine 16, another club across the street from Arena. Andy is very excited about going to this event, and believing that is a clue to something big happening on this night, I am too. Before leaving, we both take some Ecstasy and Tina. From that moment on, *this* Alice is back in Wonderland.

As we walk the few blocks to the club, the screaming returns, but very different from before. It is as if the cries are being carried to me on the gusts of the wind that blows around us. I sense Andy is hearing it too because he pauses and looks up and around. He looks at me very perplexed.

"What's wrong?" I ask.

He stares at me for a moment and then says, "Nothing."

I'm not convinced. Clearly, we both understood that that isn't true. With each gust of wind, I can hear Jeff and Seth screaming at each other. It is as though the two of them are engaged in a battle or both being tortured. I keep telling myself that none of this is real, that it is just an illusion, and nobody is really getting hurt. Defiantly, I press on.

We turn the corner and arrive at the club. There is a line forming, so we take our place and wait to purchase tickets. Andy says, "Look, there's your ugly ex."

He hates Seth. I look around and see Seth coming up the street. He looks frantic as he quickly marches past. I've seen that look in his eyes many times; I can tell there is something wrong. He is worried and angry. As I watch him, I notice Bill, a former housemate when I lived with Benjamin, walking up to me. I never cared much for that guy, especially after I discovered he was sneaking into my locked bedroom and snooping through my things. He is really creepy, Chester Molester kind of creepy.

Smiling, he asks, "What are *you* doing here?"

I don't say anything, just look at him, wondering why he is talking to me. He then says, "Do you know who's throwing this party?"

"No."

"Hmm. It's going to be a crazy night," he says and walks away.

Once inside, I pray for everything to return to normal. It is wall-to-wall bodies of hot boys and great music. But the screams continue to drift around me. Now I can hear my sister Sharon screaming too. I even think I hear my dead mother. Everyone is yelling at me, "David, no! Don't do it! No, David! Stop! David, no!"

I look around and notice groups of people talking and staring at me. Andy is now distancing himself from me. He often did this when we were at the clubs together. In the clubs, he seemed to not like me very much, and this night was no different, except for the worry in his eyes.

I pull in close and ask, "Do you want to dance?"

He scans the room and reluctantly agrees. The song booming through the sound system is "Appreciate Me," a dark gothic tribal beat, one that would be well suited to a movie with vampires and other things of the macabre. We only dance for a minute or two, until the screams and stares overwhelm me. I become really frightened, feeling like I am in a dark cave surrounded by Hell's children.

As I leave the dance floor, Seth storms up to me. He is angry and mean, the way he had been on the dance floor in Canada, after I'd survived the night's perils.

"David, I didn't do this to you. You have some kind of a family curse on you. I'm not the reason this is happening to you."

Surprised by his sudden candor, I ask, "What are you talking about?"

He just turns away. As he leaves, I notice two guys standing close by, talking and staring at me. I hear one say, "I don't know what's wrong with him. It's like he doesn't have any compassion." They too turn and walk away.

I continue to hear my family screaming for me not to do it, and I wonder what that means. I'm becoming panicked now. I walk around the club, trying to calm myself down, looking for anyone I recognize and trust. After a few minutes of this, I realize I have to get the hell out of there. As I quickly push my way to the door, those around me start laughing among themselves while pointing and staring at me.

Once outside, I head toward my apartment just a few blocks away. As I pass others walking to the club, they tease and laugh too. *How does everyone know what I am going through?* The movie, the screaming and pleading in my ears, Seth's comments, the worry Andy had, it all becomes too much. I suddenly fear that vampires or werewolves really are going to pop out at any moment and rip me to pieces. I freak out and start running.

As I run, my phone rings. It's Dominic. I have no idea why he is calling me, but sensing this call could be a lifesaver, I quickly answer. Certainly nothing bad would happen to me while on the phone. It had worked in Canada. Why not now?

"Hey Davey, what's going on?" he inquires.

Suspicious, I say, "Nothing, just walking home. I'm having a really weird night."

"I know you are," he says. "Are you okay?"

"What? How do you know what's happening?" I stop in my tracks and look around.

"I'm downtown right now, with a whole community of people praying for you."

Now I am *really* freaked out.

"It's good that you decided to go home. I'll call you later to see how you are doing. Bye," he says, his voice trailing off as the line goes dead.

I have no idea what the hell is happening, but I am taking no chances. I turn in the other direction and head straight for Jeff's. When I arrive, it feels like a rerun. He is upset that I put myself in harm's way again, but he pulls me under his wing of protection without hesitation. I am way too disturbed to climb into bed and lie motionless again, so I opt for the couch this time.

A couple of hours later, he leaves for work and I am alone again. But this time, I don't feel any safer than when I'd arrived. Too much has happened and the sketch is continuing. I can hear the familiar noises within the walls and the whispering in the air, just like the first time that I discovered I was being videotaped. I am also much more paranoid this time, not just of being watched but also of being in danger. I can't figure out what is going to happen, but I sense it is something bad.

My cell phone chimes, alerting me that a text message has arrived. It's Fred, whom I haven't talked to in quite a while. He lives two floors down. Still trusting him, I share a little of what is going on, but mostly I am relieved to be in contact with someone again. I believe nothing can happen to me if *someone* knows. He asks me to come hang out with him and talk about it. At first I refuse, but after some prodding, I give in.

I make several attempts to leave the apartment, but I can't muster the courage to unlock and open the door. I can hear people out in the hallway and in the stairwell. Just as I had been petrified with fear in that hotel in Vancouver, I am crippled with fear now. Fred sends another text message, wondering what is taking me so long. I stand there debating with myself. *Go? Don't go? Go? Don't go?*

I suddenly remember that Jeff has a gun. I go to his bedroom and pull the gun from under the mattress. I retrieve the bullets from his underwear drawer and load the chambers. Feeling empowered, I slip the gun into the front of my pants and head back to the door.

I slowly open the door and walk out into the hallway. Still feeling unbearably vulnerable, I decide to cock the hammer back and slip my finger over the trigger. My heart is pounding in my ears and chest, and every squeak compounds the fear. My cautious pace quickly becomes a run, then an all-out mad dash until I arrive at Fred's door. I pound frantically until he opens up and lets me in. My state of panic startles him. I try to play it down, a futile effort, I'm sure. Once inside, he leads me straight to his bedroom. He says he wants to lie down for a while.

With no way to avoid the awkwardness of it, I pull the gun out of my pants. He jumps back in surprise and asks, "What the hell are you doing with that?"

"I'm scared, Fred. It's for protection."

"Well, put it down! You're safe with me."

He lies down on the bed. I set the gun on the dresser, slip my shoes off, and climb into bed next to him. We are both flying on Tina, so sleep isn't happening.

I can hear Seth screaming in my ears, reacting to the deep evil rantings of the interrogator and the electric shocks he is administering. I hear a car being driven erratically. In my mind, I can see a van, and Seth is inside, being tortured by the villains with him. I hear the wheels squealing as they fly around corners, and then the engine roars as the driver smashes down on the gas. This repeats over and over. They must be in the city, probably close by.

I start to cry because something about where I am, what is happening, and what I've experienced convinces me that Seth is being killed this time.

"Why are you crying?" Fred asks.

I hesitate and then say, "I am worried about Seth. I hope he is okay."

Fred then starts revealing a story to me. It isn't verbal; he talks by typing messages into his phone for me to read. He tells me Rapture is evil, and this is happening in *her* memory, though *she* wasn't gay. He talks of a haunted satellite and says something about a fire or fireman. He gives me the impression that I'll be traveling somewhere in about 10 hours. I sense I'll be taking a long journey. I know he is preparing me for something.

We get out of bed, and he leads me through the apartment, showing me pictures of very random stuff. Collages he's made from magazine pages and assembled on the tack boards on his walls. I can see that they tell a story; I just don't understand what that story is. Next, we walk over to his computer where he shows me more curious, random stuff. I can tell he is attempting to tell me the truth about everything, but I am high, paranoid, and confused. I'm unable to connect the dots.

"Fred, I'm lost. This doesn't make any sense to me."

He looks at me and says, "It's okay, honey. I'll take care of everything. You just stay with me and I'll help you."

He then says we are going to Noc Noc, a club downtown that Seth often goes to. I've only been there a couple times. It's now around 6 am.

Fred throws together an outfit for me to wear, and we get ready to leave. Though I look better now, I am a mess on the inside. The previous 24 hours have been unimaginably sketchy. Suddenly, to my dread, I feel a heavy wave of fatigue wash over me. Oh my God, I can't fall asleep!

"Do you have any Tina?" I ask.

To my relief, Fred pulls out a mirror with a small pile of white powder. It's one thing to do drugs for recreation. It's another thing to be in a dire situation and know that ingesting this powder is going to keep you awake and alive. Afterward, we sit and wait for a friend of Fred's. In this bizarre episode, it isn't for fun.

Fred drives while I consume the G shot he prepared for me. It's in a blue coffee cup with a Superman logo emblazoned on it. He tells me his friend in the back seat is a virgin, and though I don't understand why, I know this is somehow important.

We arrive at Noc Noc and park in the lot across the street. While we are standing around near the car, talking to others and preparing to go inside, Ray pulls up with someone I don't recognize. He is surprised to see me there and becomes really suspicious when he realizes I am with Fred. He'd always been suspicious of Fred, so that in itself doesn't surprise me. Within a few minutes, he returns to normal and the awkwardness evaporates. He pulls out a camera, asks someone to snap some pictures of us, and then we head inside.

At the door, everything I witness gives me the impression something really big is being prepared for. There is a lot of commotion, with cracked-out patrons going in and out, and the doormen watching over everyone. I am treated like a rock star, an A-list celebrity, and this makes me really happy, but I'm still on guard. I sense it is all about to happen. Finally, all the pain and confusion is about to end, to be replaced by my initiation into something beyond this world. I am about to remove my rose-colored glasses forever.

Inside, the impossible continues. Fred and Ray flank both sides of me and everyone makes their rounds, pulling up to show the world they know us. I feel like the most important person who ever lived.

Then Ray disappears, and Fred leads me into the back of the club. As we cross an empty dance floor, I realize there is no music playing. This seems strange to me. At Fred's lead, we step up off the dance floor and into the back chill area.

I start to recognize some faces from my time with Seth. Those who had been treating me with hatred are now being incredibly friendly and welcoming. Off to the left I see three men sitting on a couch with several people standing around talking to them. The three men are watching me. Suddenly, the music starts. Feeling like I am under a microscope, I decide to distract myself by dancing. I return to the dance floor, and as I bounce around, I secretly watch everyone and everything, trying to calculate what is happening.

I notice Fred and some stranger talking and watching me. The expression on Fred's face worries me. He doesn't seem friendly to me now, more like an enemy plotting. Probably sensing, or flat-out knowing what I am thinking, he pulls up and hugs me, pretending nothing is happening. He points to the wall behind me. I turn and see that it is covered with a black-and-white checkered mural. The checks aren't symmetrical though; more distorted in the way varying depth would distort them. Each square is random in size, a bit like the example I have created here, though this has more of a uniform appearance to it than I remember seeing on that day.

"After today, you'll want one of these in your bathroom," he says. I have no idea what he's talking about.

We return to the back, but the three men who were sitting on the couch are gone. We sit down in their place, looking out at the rest of the club. I feel incredibly present now; time seems to be moving very slowly.

"Do you know who those men are who were sitting here?" Fred asks.

"No. I've never seen them before. Why?"

He stands, pulling with him a hoodie that was lying behind him on the couch. As he lifts it over his shoulders, like a shawl, he stares into my eyes and says, "*This is who they are.*" He turns and takes several steps away from me. On the back of the hoodie are the letters CIA. He pauses, looks over his shoulder at me, and then drops it down to his waist, hiding the letters, and slowly walks away. In that moment, my mind flashes back to a memory I had with Dominic.

I still lived with Jeff then. He had gone to bed and I was getting ready to go out with Seth. Dominic was there and had asked me for a ride. On the way, he told me that he was going to visit a man whom he knew to be a CIA agent. Apparently this man had been secretly watching Dominic and knew everything about him. He had invited Dominic over to talk with him and he would explain why he was spying on him. I never found out what happened that night.

I get up to follow Fred, but as I begin to descend the stairs onto the dance floor, I notice Seth walking toward me and I freeze. He walks slowly and confidently, looking around with a determined, powerful presence, as though he's making a statement with his presence. Everyone who notices him stops what they are doing and watches him. He is wearing a blue T-shirt with a huge metallic silver Superman logo embossed into the front. This is definitely a statement. We watch each other as he walks by. I become really angry, wondering why he is here, knowing his arrival has just changed everything. I'm happy to see that he is alive, but it hurts to realize that we have drifted apart, to know that this moment isn't happening because of our love for each other. Before, there would never have been a time when we'd arrive at the club separately. Everyone expected us to appear together, as a team. Now I realize I have no idea where he's been or what has brought him here. I doubt he suffers the same torment.

He continues to the back and settles in with his familiar group. I dance for a while, trying to shake off my anger and figure out what is happening. I eventually decide to walk back and talk to him.

I hug him and ask, "How are you?"

"I'm okay. How are you?"

"Okay, I guess."

"I was home sleeping when Ray called. I wasn't planning on coming out." He doesn't say why he decided to get out of bed and come out, but I suddenly sense he might be trying to protect me, or himself, from something that is happening.

Within minutes, an angry Fred comes up to me and says we are leaving. Confused, I say goodbye to Seth and his group, then follow Fred and his friend out of the club. The three of us climb into my car and drive away. I can tell something has completely changed the atmosphere. Fred is mean and angry now. I look back at his friend, who gives me a dirty look. I look away, and he says to Fred, "Trash here just ruined everything."

Fred looks at me and says, "I know."

I say nothing until I get Fred alone in his bedroom. "What happened, Fred? And why are you guys saying I'm trash?"

"Because you are," he says.

I crumble. I can't believe how suddenly everything has changed. I grab the gun from the dresser and say, "Fuck you." I rush down the hall and out the door, hoping to escape before the tears pour from my eyes.

Crying, I return to Jeff's, unload the gun, put it back under the mattress, and then race home. I feel hurt, confused, angry, frustrated, depressed, and so alone. God, I am so alone. My mind is flooded with memories and questions. What is happening to me? Why does everyone hate me? What did I do? Who the hell am I? Why won't anyone tell me what's going on?

I wanted to kill myself. I wanted to kill everyone else. I wanted it all to be over. I just wanted to die. The rest of the weekend I stayed home, doing my best to get through the onslaught of screams and torture. By Sunday evening I felt like I was losing my mind. Ray had brought Seth home with him, and they were trying to talk me through my sadness, but their presence offered little comfort. I blamed them for what was happening because I knew they were connected to it. I remember lying in bed sobbing hopelessly as they sat with me and poured more of their manipulating double talk into my mind. I remember wanting so desperately to push them away, to run out onto the balcony and jump, bringing all my pain to an end. But I feared that this was just the beginning of my hell, and that killing myself would ensure this misery would last for eternity.

The more they talked, the more frustrated I became until I finally exploded on them, revealing everything I felt I knew about them and their secrets. I'm not sure this was a good move, but sometimes what you know is all you have. I even told them about the night Ray fell out and I discovered that "thing" in his abdomen. I knew at that moment that they were under the spell of their secret, so I attempted to press my hands against Seth's stomach just to prove I was right. No matter what I did, they never let me touch them there, even physically restraining me to keep my hands away.

Later, they went back into the living room. I snuck out of bed and listened through the door to their whisperings. Those two were always whispering, scheming and calculating. Seth was telling Ray, "It'll be okay. It wasn't your fault. You fell out on G. They will understand."

This was one more confirmation that everything happening around me was real.

The next day, my anger grew as I struggled through my eight hours of work. Afterward, I jumped into my car and rushed home. I had left a small bag of Tina hidden just to see how thoroughly Ray was snooping through my things. He had found it of course. I realized his obsession with cleaning and rearranging my apartment was just cover for what he was really doing, watching my every move. I was on a mission now, to uncover the dark forces screwing with my life.

I'm sitting at my computer, pretending to work but really trying to put everything together. Ray is in the kitchen, high and tweaking. The screaming has returned.

"No, give him more," Ray says. With that, the screaming suddenly grows louder and more intense. I then remember what Fred had said about their secret way of communicating. An internal cell phone he called it. I had once read about such a device that could be put into a tooth filling. Then I remember Seth's statement in Canada about the incredible dental plan.

Ray disappears into the bathroom and locks the door. I know he is communicating directly with whoever is creating the horror in my ears. I put my ear to the door, and he immediately opens it.

"What are you doing?" he asks.

"I know what you're up to, Ray. I want you out of my house."

"I'm not doing anything. You're crazy."

"When I get back, you'd better be gone!"

I leave my apartment and head to Jeff's. The screaming in my ears is his voice. I need to know that he is okay. As I walk the blocks to his building, I notice everyone on the streets paying particular attention to me. I sense they are reaching out to me, letting me know that this isn't just in my head. I begin to run, believing Jeff really is being killed.

Instead, I find him sitting in a chair, curled up in a ball, crying. He doesn't seem shocked at my arrival. He tells me that I have to stop what I am pursuing, that this is affecting him more than I know. The air rushes from my lungs as I realize he is being affected in every way I had feared; I know that my suspicions are correct. I am hit with a flood of confusing memories that suddenly make complete sense. In this moment, I know they have gotten to him. I'm suddenly aware that I no longer have anyone to help me escape this hell. I know they have gotten to the only person who can help me get away from them.

I look into his eyes. Tears run down my face and promise him I won't hurt him. I turn and run out the door, down the five flights of stairs, out to the street, and head home. With each step, I hear Jeff scream louder and louder, as though each step brings him more and more pain.

As freaked out as I am, I believe that every step I take is causing him harm. I stop and turn back. I then notice someone looking out a window at me, from the apartment building across the street. He points to me, and laughing says, "Look, he's going back!" I pause; he laughs. I turn back; he laughs. I hear others laughing too. I run full speed back to Jeff.

Across the street from Jeff's building is a bar, and from the windows I hear laughter and see people pointing at me through the windows, making fun of my fear. I scream, "FUCK YOU!" as I run, but that only increases the laughing and hysteria. When I run into Jeff's apartment, he is in bed, crying. He seems startled this time. He notices how frightened I am, but he still becomes angry with me. I can't understand it. Why is he pushing me away? I begin to cry again and run out the door. I run without stopping all the way to my apartment. I am alone.

I crawl into bed and cry. But I can't block out the screaming of Jeff and Seth. It sounds like they are killing each other. Seth is yelling that they are killing Jeff, that they are causing him to have a heart attack. Because of the electric shocks, it makes sense to me. I force myself to lie there, repeating to myself that this isn't real, that they are just trying to scare me. But I can't lie there and listen to Jeff die. I finally crack and run out the door and back to Jeff.

Along the way I see many people coming out on the streets. Some look like they are there to help by witnessing my journey, keeping me from being alone for even an instant, and others to hurt, like they are hoping for a perfect moment to take me out. With each shady character that appears, so does another that looks friendly.

I am so frightened, I run in the middle of the street to avoid anyone getting close enough to hurt me.

It is late now. So when I enter Jeff's apartment, he jumps out of bed, startled awake. When he realizes it is me, he becomes angry again. I start crying, telling him how afraid I am that he is being hurt. He instantly shifts from anger to sadness. He tells me to get into bed with him and stay the night. By then, after several trips back and forth, I know the only way I'll be satisfied with his safety is to be by his side.

I could have never been prepared for what happened next. Nobody could ever be prepared to listen to a loved one get murdered. On this night, as I lie in bed losing my mind, I listen to members of my family being slaughtered, one by one. I hear a gang of criminals driving from house to house, mutilating my nieces and nephews. I hear their screams of struggle and those of their mothers, my sisters, discovering that their children are dead.

I hear Robin saying to her little girl, "Megan, what's wrong?" and Megan reply, "Mommy, I hear somebody in the house." Then I hear Robin say, "Oh God, run, Megan!" Then I hear gunshots. Next comes the squealing of tires as the evil bastards drive away, followed by police cars arriving on the scene. I hear Sharon's wails as John tell her Robin is dead. Then I hear the monsters arriving at the next house, that of my nephew. I hear chainsaws, followed by cars again speeding away. I hear my other sister screaming, "Oh my God, they cut his head off!"

It is like watching a horror movie with my eyes closed, except it was my family. I keep trying to get out of bed, but Jeff holds me in bed and tells me to try and sleep, pleading with me to try and ignore it. Not because it is in my head, but because it is pointless to do anything but lie there and take it.

The next morning, Jeff comforted me and encouraged me to go on about my day as best as possible. Because of his calm demeanor, I knew that none of what I'd listened to during the night had really happened, I knew that my family hadn't really died, even though I knew we had both listened to all of it. I was a wreck and hadn't slept, but he knew I had to go to work. My attendance had suffered greatly because of all this craziness, so missing work would have meant losing my job. As I got ready and drove to work, the terror continued in my ears. I kept thinking about what Jeff said about being strong. I managed to get through a few hours at work, until finally I could take no more. The constant screaming and horror of hearing my loved ones dying over and over, of hearing Seth and Jeff getting tortured continually was too much. I searched desperately in the faces of my coworkers, most of whom were strangely away from their workstations on this day, leaving me alone in my department, and when they were around, it seemed as though everyone was doing their best to pretend nothing was happening, but the way they would look around, with that worry in their faces, as they walked through the department, if felt impossible to me that they weren't hearing what I was. One of them, as he walked through, looked up and around, and then at me and said, "Jesus Christ." I fell apart, crying and ran out of the building.

And with that, I lost my job. I raced home, crying all the way. In my rear-view mirror, I noticed someone from work following me. It was our IT tech, Kim. I think he was following to make sure I was okay. As I weaved through traffic, he followed my every move. This made me to slow down and drive more carefully. About half way home, he sped up past me, looking at me as he went by, and then exited.

When I got home, I called Jeff to tell him what had happened. I was still under attack and terrified. I was out on my balcony, smoking and crying, doing my best to stave off a complete mental break. I was so weary, feeling worn down and helpless, thinking about suicide again. I just wanted the screaming in my ears to stop. I wanted everything to end, including my life.

I remember looking out from my balcony, seeing all the people moving about their apartments, hearing the cars and buses whizzing past, and wondering why I was so alone. Why was nobody doing anything to help me?

At last I stood up, grabbed the railing, leaned out, and screamed, "Doesn't anyone see what's happening to me? Why won't anyone help me? Why won't you help me? God damn it, somebody please help me! I hate this fucking city!"

I then climbed into bed and cried myself to sleep, the only place I could escape to. When he got off work, Jeff came over to my place, crawled into bed with me, and held me close. When I woke up several hours later, he was gone.

A few days later, things slowly returned to a relative level of normalcy and the voices finally faded away. Though I couldn't talk to my family, Jeff assured me that everyone was fine. I called and talked to my boss. He was concerned about me and what I was going through, but he couldn't offer my job back. He gave me one final piece of advice before letting me go. He said, "David, remember this. What doesn't kill you only makes you stronger." Luckily, I secured another job one week later.

The Tide is Shifting

As all of this was happening, forces were coming together that would help me to finally escape this madness once and for all, though it would be at least another six months until I felt like I had completely pulled from the grip that world had over me.

During this time, Dominic was starting to become a presence in my life. He and I started to spend time together, becoming friends. We also had a strong attraction for each other, but he was still seeing Jeff a little, and I was still seeing Andy. He did seem to know and understand a lot of what and why things were happening to me, and I grabbed onto that.

A week or so later, about the third week of October, Dominic called and asked if he could stay the night at my place. He was on the hill and didn't have a way home. The next morning I had to work, so I gave him my key and left him there. Ray was still staying with me and was asleep on the couch.

Later that morning I received a call from Dominic. He was really upset, crying. He said he and Ray were arguing and Ray had slapped him across the face. I told him I would come home at lunchtime, instructed him to lock himself in my room, and call Jeff. I knew Seth and Ray hated him, so it didn't surprise me that something like this would happen.

A couple hours later I received a call from Jeff. He was at my apartment. After talking to Dominic, he had gone there and attempted to kick Ray out. I immediately raced home to find the police were there too. Ray had called the police and was trying to have Jeff arrested for assault. It was a very ugly situation, one that put me in the position of having to choose sides.

I wasn't sure what exactly had taken place, but I did know one thing for sure, I trusted Jeff. I had had over a decade to get to know this man and I knew I trusted him with my life. As for Seth, Ray, and that whole mess? I knew this hell started when they came into my life. My decision was easy to make. And once I spoke the words, the officers told Ray to collect his things and leave. He tried desperately to convince them that Jeff was the bad one and he should be arrested, but the officers saw right through his ruse, warning him to drop it or risk being arrested himself.

It didn't take Seth long to discover what had happened, and when he did, he blamed me for everything. I tried to get him to see the truth, but as always, he could only see what he wanted to, so with that, he cut off contact with me.

The following weekend, I was once again suffering under the audible torture. This one was different though. It started quietly. I heard a door open and then Ray talking to someone. Then he yelled, "Get your hands off me!" Next, I heard him getting knocked around and being yelled at. It quickly escalated into a full torture session, just as I'd heard Seth and Jeff go through many times before. This went on for several hours. Powerless to stop it, all I could do was hunker down in my apartment and do my best to get through it.

It's Sunday afternoon now. Sitting on my balcony smoking a cigarette, I hear Andy's voice. I peek over the railing and see him standing below, talking to three other guys I have seen around the property several times. They often attend the many sex parties the manager hosts on weekends. I learned that Andy was also a frequent guest of those parties.

I hide there and listen to their conversation, hoping to find out something about Andy and why he is in my life. One of the guys says, "Man, what's the deal with Ray? Why are they being so rough on him?"

"So that it never happens again," Andy replies.

Then another guy says, "My god, it sounds really bad."

Their conversation is glum. They then talk about some trip everyone is planning. I can tell they are discussing logistics of some sort, but when I accidentally make a noise, they look up and stop talking. I go back into my apartment, thinking Andy is on his way to see me, but he never calls or shows up.

After hearing that conversation, I knew for sure why Ray was being hurt, and importantly, I knew that he really was being hurt. I'm sure this was happening because of the discovery I had made in his abdomen that night.

With Seth and Ray out of my life, Jeff started spending more time with me. His love and concern for me once again revealed itself as he helped me try to put my life back together. He helped me get a handle on my finances and prepare for bankruptcy. He held my hand while I purchased a used Honda Civic so I could let my 350Z go back to the finance company. As frightening and painful as it was, he encouraged me to be strong and keep going. And he made me laugh a little too, something I did very little in those dark days. I had nearly lost my trust in him during this time, as I had for everyone in my life then. I had begun to wonder if he had become one of them. I knew that everyone knew what I was going through, but nobody would admit it, nor did it seem like anyone was trying to help me. But my long history with Jeff, and the way he was helping me now, so selflessly, gave me something to hold onto to. I wasn't entirely convinced that he hadn't been compromised, but I needed someone to help me pull myself back together, and he was the only person I could hold on to.

About a month after Seth had stopped talking to me, I receive a call from him. It is early in the morning, and I am getting ready for work. He is really upset.

"I'm sorry for calling you, but I had nobody else."

"It's okay. What's wrong?"

"My car got towed last night. Will you give me a ride to get it?"

"Yea, sure. When?"

"Now? I'm already late for work. I can meet you out front."

"Okay. Give me 10 minutes."

As I pull up to him, he doesn't recognize me at first because I'm in a different car. He opens the door and climbs in.

"When did you get this?" he asks.

"A couple weeks ago. I had to let my Z go back. I couldn't afford it anymore."

Tears begin to well up in his eyes. He looks away and I pull away from the curb. We drive in silence for a few blocks.

"How are you doing?" he asks.

"I'm okay, I guess. Are you doing okay?"

He begins to cry again, shaking his head no.

I'm careful not to reveal too much of what a struggle each day is for me, but I'm sure he knows. He tries desperately to hold back the tears.

When we arrive at the towing company, he thanks me and quickly gets out. As I drive away, I begin to cry, and I continue to cry all the way to work. After all I've been through, all he's put me through, and with all the questions I still have, I am still in love with him. And it seems like he is too.

So, we started talking again. And we started courting each other again. Crazy, I know. But it was very short-lived. It never took long until the arguing returned. I suppose that had its purpose, just as everything else seems to have had.

Right away, Seth told me something about Ray. After Ray left my place, he stayed with Seth for a while. During that time, Ray's parents had come to visit, just showing up at Seth's door one day, without any notice. They lived in South Dakota. Seth explained how strange it was, how they just showed up unannounced. He said that they were really despondent during the few days they were there, and that his mother cried a lot.

After Seth shared all the details of those days, I was left with the impression that they somehow knew something bad was going to happen to Ray. I don't know if they were there to try to prevent it, or if they were there to say goodbye to him. I definitely understood that Ray was in mortal danger. And knowing what I had listened to that day in my apartment, I believe the torture I heard him going through must have been real. Seth then blamed me for what happened to him and started in on everything else he was still pissed about. And the arguing began again.

While away from him, I had compiled some notes about all the facts I knew, trying to find answers. I decided to share these with him, to show him what I knew, to try and prove that none of this was my fault. He looked surprised, at first saying he felt very sorry for me, and not sorry in a nice way. But as we argued, he suddenly changed tactics and instead of blaming me, he said he wanted to help me. He seemed so frustrated and kept saying I was caught in a loop, like a computer program.

"David, you are so close," he said. "You've almost got it. But you need to step back and look at it in a different way."

In moments like this, I could see glimpses of the original Seth I'd met long ago, the one I trusted, the one I believed really loved me. We then cried together and he said he'd continue to help me but with one caveat. As always, he said he needed to be in complete control. And so continued the other endless loop we were stuck in.

He was only back in my life for a few weeks, but some interesting things happened during that time. One night while we were sitting on his couch watching TV, he was rubbing my neck. When he pushed on one spot, he heard a clicking sound.

"What is that?" he asks.

"I don't know, but it's always done that."

"That's not normal. You should find out what that is."

A little while later he asks, "What do you think about aliens?"

"What? Aliens? I don't know. I'm sure they exist, but I haven't thought about it much."

He then pushes on my neck again and when it clicks, says, "You really should find out what that is." I dismiss it as him trying to sketch me out.

During this time, I decided to get some help with my drug use. Though I wasn't doing them as much as I had been, I was still using on the weekends, mostly because of how horny it made me and how I looked forward to the many hours of self-pleasure that would come with being high. I knew this wasn't normal or healthy behavior, and afterward, I would fall into a deep depression because of it.

I realized it was time to stop completely, but I needed help. Through my therapist Michael, I got in touch with a counselor at NEON, a drug recovery program offered through Seattle Counseling Services for the LGBT community. Seth tried to discourage me, lobbying that it was okay to use drugs. But by then, I didn't put much stock into what he said. I knew I had an addictive problem with drugs, and I was beginning to understand my addiction to him.

In my first meeting with the counselor, I learned more about Seth and his associates than I ever imagined I would. Well, it was more of a confirmation really. After listening to what I described, he confirmed that these people were involved in something very bad. He knew about their club, and he said that several of his counseling clients had been preyed upon by these people in the same way I had been. Seth was a member of this club, just as many of his friends were, I could finally accept that these people weren't my friends and what was happening to me was really bad. Hearing it so soberly from this counselor, I knew I had finally found something to grasp onto, a rope that was going to pull me out of the hell I was swimming in. Though it would be several weeks before I completely stopped using drugs, I was on my way.

It's interesting that almost overnight from that time on my balcony when I screamed for help, forces started falling into place to help me. In a very literal sense, when I asked for it, help arrived. Slowly but surely the tide was changing, and step by step things were beginning to get better for me.

Silver Clouds

It's Saturday night, a few weeks before Christmas. Dominic is over. While he sleeps in my bedroom, I sit awake in the living room listening to a CD Seth had given me. It is a compilation of dance music created by a local DJ we know. Something in the lyrics catches my attention. I realize there is an underlying story within the entire CD. I listen to it over and over, bewildered by what I am hearing. The lyrics are about the secret and the pleasure it brings.

Remembering that the CD case has a song list printed inside it, I pull it out and jump onto the Internet and start Googling song names, artists, and lyrics. One thing leads to the next until I have discovered several websites that seem to know about the secret. I can't believe how well hidden, in plain sight, everything is. I research all night until Dominic stops me.

As I'm sitting there obsessively reading and searching, I happen to glance to my right, and there he is, his head inches from mine, reading what is on my screen. Startled, I jump and yell, "Dominic! You scared the crap out of me!"

Without looking away from the screen, he says, "What are you doing, Davey?"

"Nothing. Just looking up stuff."

He looks at me with concern and says, "David, that stuff is sketchy. You shouldn't be looking at that."

He grabs my mouse and closes the windows. "Let's go Christmas shopping." He turns my chair away from the computer and says, "Go, get ready."

Fast forward to later in the day. We're downtown, walking within the river of bundled-up shoppers on Pine Street, and heading west toward Nordstrom. Dominic seems distracted, lost in thought, probably listening to the voice in his head. The literal voice in his head. Suddenly he says, "Let's go have a Martini. I know this place that makes a great Martini."

I agree, not understanding what is really going on. So we turn in the other direction and walk up Pine Street to an Asian café a few blocks away. Once inside, I immediately sense the energy of the people inside—a dark, profound sadness. As the host leads us back to our table, everyone who looks at us seems crestfallen. From our table I watch the staff moving about and the patrons sitting around us. Everyone's energy is so heavy I can feel it pressing down on me. I don't understand what is happening, and it begins to overwhelm me.

I know something is happening, but I can't figure out what it could possibly be. I suppose it was the inevitable result of this long, painful journey of mine, an end that was destined to be.

When the waiter returns to take our order, Dominic takes the lead and orders for us. "We'll both be having the Silver Cloud Martini," he says. I continue to notice how sad everyone seems, including Dominic now too. My monster stirs to life.

When our cocktails arrive, I am surprised to see martini glasses filled with what looks like metallic silver paint suspended in a clear liquid. I know immediately this drink holds secrets.

Feeling uneasy, I ask Dominic, "Is this going to hurt me?"

Sarcastically, he responds, "It's full of glass that's going to cut you up on the inside. Cheers!" He taps his glass to mine and takes a drink. After watching him swallow, I slowly lift my glass, stare into the swirling silver cloud, and hesitantly put it to my lips. As the silver-laced alcohol pours into my mouth, I notice the tears rolling down Dominic's face. I think of the words from a poem Ricky had given me, "It's coming to America first/because we have the machinery/It's coming on a flood of alcohol."

After our drink, Dominic calls Jeff. Though we haven't done any shopping yet, he says we should go see him. Jeff is volunteering on the Christmas tree lot for SASG, an HIV/AIDS organization. When we show up, I instantly realize Jeff isn't happy. The glare he pours over Dominic confirms to me that he knows what has happened and is very upset about it. As quickly as he flashes his anger at Dominic, he switches into his familiar unconditional love for me.

The other people on the lot aren't so capable of hiding their anger. When I ask Dominic about the vexation I am detecting within the faces of those around us, he hugs me, pulls my face next to his, and looks out at them with a trophy confidence, and assures me they don't understand.

Realizing our welcome is thin at best, Dominic forces our goodbyes and we quickly leave. Our next stop is the Manray Video Bar. It is the post 5 o'clock cocktail hour and the place is busy with lost souls. We grab a table and order another round of martinis, though these don't have the mysterious ingredient our earlier libation had included. Becoming intoxicated on alcohol and attention, Dominic flicks his Paris Hilton switch and becomes a gay boy magnet, his favorite thing to be. I park myself in a chair, trying my best to portray wallpaper so that I can process the day's events, my most comfortable place to be.

I didn't realize how incredibly compromised I'd been when I downed that Silver Cloud, but minute by minute as the night progresses, I realize what a huge mistake I have made. As I sit there watching Dominic working his magic on the table of boys and fag hags next to us, I became overwhelmed by regret. In a sudden explosion of awareness, my mind connects the dots and I know why everyone was so upset. The Silver Cloud Martini did contain something secret, and with it now inside me, it is too late to do anything about it. The nano-seed has been planted.

Suddenly, nothing about this mysterious life matters to me, for I now know it is all a lie. Everything I thought I knew, all that I see in the world around me is just illusion. A story told to us to keep us comfortably numb. I watch the comatose souls bumping around in a drunken mess, their only concerns are their Abercrombie outfits and getting laid. They know nothing about the real world, and they don't even question the hypnotized slumber they have accepted as truth.

I am overcome by a powerful anxiety attack. Each heartbeat and string of thought builds a stronger and stronger hyperventilation, tears fill my eyes and fear fills my heart, until I finally jump to my feet and run out the door.

I stand outside trying to shake the darkness off me like a cat does water. Almost without hesitation, I jump into my car and speed to Seth, a few blocks away. I need love and trust and ironically, he is the one I run to. I need someone who knows exactly what is happening to me. I know he does. When I get there, I pound on his window, then jump down the steps and pound on his door. He quickly answers, seeming to anticipate my arrival. I throw my arms around him and melt into a deep cry.

As rapidly as I can, I tell him of the day's events. I am tired and frightened, but I need him to know what is happening. I put my arms around him and hold him close to me, and doing so brings back every memory I have of loving him and him loving me. The love I feel for him is overwhelming. *God, why am I so in love with him?*

It always feels so wonderful to wrap my arms around him and just stay there. I look into his eyes and crying hysterically, I tell him I now know what it is all about. Sobbing, I say, "Seth, I don't want to know what I know. Why didn't you stop me?"

"Baby, I tried."

He holds me and cries with me. He asks me to stay the night with him. As I lie there in bed, unable to sleep, so much goes through my mind. I try to make sense of what has happened.

And I listen to the screaming. This is the first time it has ever happened with Seth present. I try to understand how I ended up in Seth's bed of all places. I hear a van outside the window in the parking lot, and there is a boy inside, screaming in pain. I worry about someone planting a dead body in my car parked nearby. Getting set up for something I hadn't done becomes a huge worry. I have a sense that they pulled into this lot at this moment to show me that they could, to terrorize me. I hear them screaming at him and threatening him. As I hear them in my head, I hear something happening in the parking lot just outside Seth's window. Somehow, it's all connected.

Interestingly on this night, I never hear Seth screaming in agony, even though he was always part of the torture I heard. But not tonight, not as he lay next to me sleeping.

When the sun finally begins to rise, I get the hell out of there. As I approach my car, I cautiously look inside, praying that none of what I had listened to the night before has really happened. There are no dead bodies inside. I jump in and drive myself home to get ready for work. It is strange, even though I haven't slept a wink in three days, my head is clear and I feel surprisingly normal, except for the boy screaming in my ears.

As I focus on my job and enjoy the relief of my surprisingly clear mind, I begin to wonder if the boy I hear screaming is Dominic. Recognizing his voice, I immediately become concerned for him.

The minute my lunch break arrives, I decide to visit Dominic at his job. He works just three blocks from where I do. To my relief, he is okay. We visit outside, sharing a cigarette together. I am bursting with energy, something he seems happily intrigued by. Is it an effect of the Silver Cloud? There has never been a time when I'd been up for days without the help of drugs and not felt crippled by an overwhelming sense of fatigue, insecurity, and paranoia. Hell, if I drink too much coffee, I become a nervous nelly. But not today.

Now I Can See

The following day is my weekly scheduled appointment with Michael. This meeting is different though. As I sit in the waiting area, I hear some commotion in his office. It sounds as though he is upset, yelling at someone. After a few minutes, a man emerges, with a rolled up set of papers in his hand. I look up at him and smile, but he glares back at me as he slowly walks through the door. A few minutes later, Michael invites me in.

His eyes are very red and he seems upset. He apologizes for what I might have overheard, saying something about talking to himself. I sense that this stranger who walked out ahead of me has just opened his eyes.

I tell him about my adventures with Dominic. I am concerned that whatever I'd consumed in the Silver Cloud is going to harm me in some way, but I also feel somehow happy about it. It feels like a breakthrough, a lucky event that somehow changed everything, but how I don't yet know.

A week or so after the Silver Cloud, I developed an incredible new ability. While lying in bed one night trying to fall asleep, I noticed something unexpected happening within me. Using my mind, I was suddenly able to create waves of energy and move them around within my body. It was a strange but curiously pleasurable feeling. I would focus my attention on different areas and there would be a reaction there. After a little time playing with it, I discovered that I could stimulate myself sexually using only my mind. As though an invisible hand were masturbating my penis, I could feel the blood rushing back and forth, arousing me to a full erection, and then it ended with a surprisingly powerful orgasm.

Afterward, I lay there in a profound euphoria, bewildered by what had just happened. My mind flooded with memories of everything I'd been through. I thought about Seth and all the painful and confusing events I'd experienced while I was with him. I thought about the secret I'd discovered and I knew absolutely that this was a huge piece of that puzzle. I also thought about the ramifications of what this technology could mean to the individuals it touched. I wondered if this might not be the micro-chipping of society the conspiracy theorists talk of. It would certainly explain much of the craziness I'd been through. In the end, I can't say for sure what it all means.

It takes incredible concentration to bring myself to such heights of pleasure using this new gift. I did notice by chance that it was much easier to control if I smoked a little pot before. And that got me to thinking. What if there existed a device, a technology that could do the thinking for me, say something using Bluetooth or a similar form of communication? Now that would really be something incredible. And with that thought, suddenly everything started to make a lot of sense to me.

What seemed to me to be a result of my consuming the Silver Cloud, Michael and Jeff's concern for my welfare suddenly peaked. They became adamant that I end my ties with Seth. Jeff went so far as to attend my next therapy session, and together Michael and Jeff performed a desperate intervention to convince me to end my relationship with Seth once and for all. In that moment, because of all that had happened, I somehow knew I had to do this, I knew it was time. I wondered if the Silver Cloud had changed everything. When we walked out of that session, to Jeff's surprise, I called T-Mobile and immediately changed my cell number. In that step, I was done and it was over. And for good measure, I ended my relationship with Andy shortly after.

It didn't take long for Seth to kick into desperation, trying to get a hold of me, to keep me from doing what had to be done. He called my apartment repeatedly, leaving message after message on the landline I kept for faxing my clients. "David, what are you doing? You need to call me. You can't do this." He emailed continually, and eventually even arrived at my door, trying to get me to answer. But after several days of this, he stopped. Other than a quick chat months later, we have never spoken to each other again.

Goodbye Seth, hello Dominic. And was this any better? Jeff didn't object and neither did Michael, so I didn't worry about it too much. I initially saw Dominic's presence in my life as a blessing. I credited him as being the springboard that helped me heal from my breakup with Seth. Or better said, he provided me with the cushion I needed to get over Seth. I don't know if I would have been able to let go of Seth had my heart not been distracted by Dominic. My relationship with him was so distracting that I didn't much think about Seth anymore. I was falling in love again, and this was what I needed to escape the power Seth held over me. Today, I wonder, was it designed that way? There were always the signs that tried to tell me about Dominic and his allegiances to these people. Surely, after so many years of that secret perfecting itself, little old me couldn't have surprised anyone. Or did I? I do believe they thought it best to get rid of me, whatever that meant. I believe they would have preferred I kill myself. Suicide can be blamed on nobody but the victim. And dead men don't talk. Fortunately, I never succeeded.

My six months with Dominic were very eye-opening, exciting, dramatic, and heartbreaking. When he wasn't tearing my heart out, I wanted to smother him with my love. Yes, he was a train wreck of a boyfriend, but I'm sure I was a bit of mess too. All in all, we did have a lot of fun together, but it would end badly, just as my time with Seth did.

I learned a lot from Dominic. He didn't seem to have the same agenda that Seth did. He didn't use his secret to hurt me the way Seth did. But I did learn some things about that secret while we were together. Well, I guess I received confirmation of many of the strange events that I'd experienced with Seth. At various times, he displayed the same sexual pleasure, and on occasion, the same bouts of pain.

Aliens were continually abducting Dominic, or so he said. On his birthday, he disappeared from my house. With all his friends present, he just vanished. We sat on the front porch waiting, and eventually, he came strolling down the middle of the street, without shoes or socks. He had no explanation, other than having been abducted. He never deviated from that explanation. This made me think of what Seth had asked me about aliens.

As a confirming testament to what I'd experienced with Seth and once with Jeff, one night while partying at Dominic's, his friend picked up his Palm Pilot, pointed it at me, mock-pushed a button, and said, "Do you realize this is a deadly weapon?"

Knowing full well what she was saying, I grabbed it from her hands, pointed it at Dominic, and said, "Bzzt, you're dead, bitch."

His eyes grew as large as saucers, and then he ripped the pilot from my hands and angrily said, "That's sketchy. Don't do that."

Among the many moments of enlightening times with Dominic, there were plenty of heart-breaking events that eventually shook me from my love-glazed stupor. His uncontrollably drifting attention to girls and boys, and sloppy attempts to hide it, finally brought this chapter of my life to an end, albeit a dramatic end. Drama until the very end, Mary!

One Saturday night, after clubbing with my friend Heli, I decide to pop in on Dominic. It was innocent enough; I was a little tipsy and missing his touch. Things hadn't been good between us for a while. Being the hopeless lover I was, I just needed to touch him to know everything would eventually be better between us.

When I pull up to his apartment building, I notice the car of one of his coworkers parked out front. She is an older lady with a dark aura who is into astrology and cult-like figures. Dominic once told me about her past relationship with a cult leader whom she was now running from.

After ringing several times without answer, I become angry, knowing his bisexual ways and his attraction to her. I know if her car is there, he is too. I wait at the door hoping somebody might come and I'd think of a clever ploy to be let in. But it is 2 am, and nobody comes.

In the pouring rain, I decide to walk around to the back of the building, the side his unit is on. I look up five stories and notice that the only lights on are his. I become determined to discover what the hell is going on. Wonder-twin super-powers activate! I channel and become Spiderman.

I leap to the first balcony, brace myself, and then reach up to the railing of the next. With a deep breath, a swing, strategic foot placement, and a reach, I pull myself up to the next balcony. I repeat this over and over until I arrive at my destination.

Feeling suddenly awkward, I look inside before pulling myself onto his balcony. When I realize he is lying next to someone on his futon, making out, I know I have not made a mistake.

I jump onto the balcony, place my hand upon the handle, take a deep breath, rip the door open, and burst inside. At first I get no response; they don't even notice me. *Shit.* So I walk over to them, bend over to within a foot of their heads, and say, "Hello, bitches!" Now I have their full attention.

The next three hours are a blur of drama. My heart is undeniably broken, and I begin with the strength of a woman scorned. Until the part where I tuck him into bed, hold him close for several hours, and then make sure he gets to work on time the next morning.

It took about another week to convince myself that it was time to be done with all of this. Fighting my aching heart, I managed to finally break up with Dominic in the parking lot where I worked. I'll never forget watching him walk away, then pause and look back at me with a genuine surprise that I was really kissing him goodbye. I wanted to run to him and throw my arms around him, but I knew I couldn't. I just watched, numb, as he slowly walked away.

I returned to my desk and began to bawl my eyes out. I felt the full brunt of how destructive this entire period of two years had been to my heart and my life. I felt helpless, shattered, and angry. I couldn't understand why my life had become so devastated.

Just as I was about to fall into a rage of despair, ready to spill my pain onto everyone around me, my inbox chimed with a new message. I wiped my tears away and clicked on a message from my good buddy John Steers. In another turn of all the unbelievable turns of my life, this click of the mouse ushered in the next amazing period of my journey, an ascension filled with love, healing, and the welcoming of me back to a healthy and protected way of living. With beautiful Grace, I received a final confirmation that something much bigger than me was at play in my life. Upon reading his words, I realized I had never been alone, never would be, and I suddenly understood how blessed I truly am. Here's what he said:

"I never did stop singing your song."

YOUR SONG ...

When a woman in a certain African tribe knows she is pregnant, she goes into the wilderness with a few friends and together they pray and meditate until they hear the song of the child.

They recognize that every soul has its own vibration that expresses its unique flavor and purpose. When the women attune to the song, they sing it out loud. Then they return to the tribe and teach it to everyone else.

When the child is born, the community gathers and sings the child's song to him or her. Later, when the child enters school, the village gathers and chants the child's song. When the child passes through the initiation to adulthood, the people again come together and sing. At the time of marriage, the person hears his or her song.

Finally, when the soul is about to pass from this world, the family and friends gather at the person's bed, just as they did at their birth, and they sing the person to the next life.

In this African tribe, there is one other occasion upon which the villagers sing to the child. If at any time during his or her life, the person commits a crime or aberrant social act, the individual is called to the center of the village and the people in the community form a circle around him or her. Then they sing the song.

The tribe recognizes that the correction for antisocial behavior is not punishment; it is love and the remembrance of identity.

When you recognize your own song, you have no desire or need to do anything that would hurt another. A friend is someone who knows your song and sings it to you when you have forgotten it. Those who love you are not fooled by the mistakes you have made or dark images you hold about yourself. They remember your beauty when you feel ugly, your wholeness when you are broken, your innocence when you feel guilty, and your purpose when you are confused.

You may not have grown up in an African tribe that sings your song to you at crucial life transitions, but life is always reminding you when you are in tune with yourself and when you are not. When you feel good, what you are doing matches your song, and when you feel awful, it doesn't.

In the end, we shall all recognize our song and sing it well.

You may feel a little wobbly sometimes, but so have all the great singers. Just keep singing and you'll find your way home.

September 2007

It has been nearly four years since I walked away from Seth and the toxic world that he introduced to me. Nearly six years have passed since all of that madness began, and what a difference time has made. Or maybe it's this daunting path of speaking my truth that has brought about the changes I've so longed for. Maybe it has been the love and support I've received from so many in my life today. Maybe it is all of these elements combined. I'm just happy to be here. My head is clear, my life is calm, and my system has been clean of drugs and sketch for years now. I have lived, loved, learned, and recovered, and I am now a stronger, better person because of it. I am a peaceful warrior.

I think part of the reason I am feeling some genuine peace in my soul is because I finally know who I am. And finally, I am my friend. I don't hate myself anymore. I think I've hated me for most of my life. But when I had to fight to keep myself alive, something in me began to change. It was the beginning of a long road of healing the hatred I held for myself.

Today, I love who I am and I will protect myself from anything and anyone that sets out to hurt me. And even when I think for a moment that I am alone, I know I am not. None of us ever are. I know that I have everyone who really loves me, and they will always be by my side. I now know that when you love who you are, you are never alone, for you have a best friend with you always.

Not long ago, my cat managed to tumble halfway down the 200-foot cliff that is my backyard. He then somehow traversed 30 feet of dense blackberry vines and finally climbed 15 feet up a tree where he became stuck. He had been there all night. I suspect he was escaping his own demise by some unknown wild animal. Many cats have disappeared in these parts due to coyotes and raccoons. It wasn't until the next day, when he didn't return home, that I knew something was wrong. When I called out for him, I was immediately greeted with his cries of distress.

After much distress of my own, I realized I had to rescue him. Jeff and my wonderful neighbor Rich lowered me down the cliff, secured to a rope, and from there I hung on while whacking a path through the thorny vines to get to the tree. I then climbed that tree, wrested him free, and slowly made my way back. I managed to survive his frightened claw-swiping attacks while battling those of the blackberry to finally climb back up the rope and delivery him to safety and the anxious gathering of my neighbors. I then collapsed in complete exhaustion. It had been a three-hour rescue.

The point of this story is this: Before I grabbed that rope and headed down that cliff, Jeff assessed the situation and, out of concern for me, said I shouldn't do it. My only response, because it was the only one available to me, was, "What, do I just let him die? I don't have a choice. I have to save him."

And that is how I feel about my life. I just have to keep going. Be strong, love myself and those who love me, but *keep going*. God will let me know when it's time to let go. Until then, I must keep going.

Before I began writing this book, I wondered if I'd ever recover from it all. My spirit had been broken and I lived suffering under the pain of what had happened, replaying the memories over and over, searching for the answers that would satisfy me. My life felt haunted and my soul ached to understand what I'd been through. I began to think that nothing would undo the hurt to allow me to move beyond the mystery of what was. Though I knew the telling of my story should happen, I was afraid for too long to tell it. Even though I had escaped the talons of that dark world, I worried that somehow they were still with me, watching, listening.

I talked myself into thinking that I should keep silent and never again mention what had happened. And I stayed with that fear for a long time. But as time went on, and because of the pain that continued to haunt my life, I knew it wasn't the right thing for me to do. So, I searched within the world around me for answers. I read book after book after book; I poured through thousands of websites, listened to many lectures, and watched many movies. I listened to the stories of other people, and through it all, I always held my experiences up to the light, using them as my guide to finding truth. In doing so, I answered many questions I had about what I'd lived through. I feel I now understand much of what came into my life during that dark time.

Do I believe that this mysterious sexual technology has origins from beyond our world? I don't know for sure, though I have strong theories about it. If our governments had to admit to the world that we are not alone in the universe, would they think this knowledge would throw the belief systems and religions of everyone on this planet into chaos? And why is it that the criminal underworld has such access to this technology? Maybe it is the tool that helps them enforce their *omerta*, their code of silence. Maybe it is the seductive tool they use to recruit. Maybe Rapture is evil, being manipulated by an elite group of souls on this planet. Maybe this is the knowledge that bonds the mafia and the governments of the world.

What is that clicking thing in my neck? Is it some type of microchip? Do we live in a society that microchips everyone at birth?

I may never know the answers to these questions definitively. But for me, these questions were birthed during the nightmare I lived through. The answers to these questions will be hard to find—and even harder to accept for anyone who hasn't been through what I have. Had I not lived through these incredible events of my life, I would likely struggle to believe that any of it could be anything other than conspiracy theories or fantasy.

But the truth is, I have found glimpses of the answers in what I've experienced and discovered. There are some very strange things happening in this world. My only advice is to question everything. In the end, only you can decide for yourself what you are ready to believe. In the end, we each must choose our reality.

I wrote my story, just as it happened for me, because I believe it is a story that needs to be shared with the world. In taking this, what feels like the final step, my last hope to overcome the hurt and pain, I came to realize that silence does equal death, and that no, I shouldn't keep my mouth shut. I realized it's only when the light of truth is shone upon the darkness that the darkness is defeated. To stay silent, you keep the darkness. This is what has allowed the darkness to endure for so long, the silence.

This journey has completely changed me as a person in ways that I could never have imagined. It has been an awakening that has revealed a deeper, more beautiful way of seeing and experiencing this life. No longer do I feel hopelessly alone and afraid. In fact, I know I'll never be alone again. This world, this universe, every inch of everything is here to show us that we are spirit, we are loved, and we are eternal. We are one, all of us God. There should be no fear and no judgment, just forgiveness and love. But with that comes a responsibility to live honestly and generously, loving and nurturing all that exists around us, including ourselves. We need to pay attention to what's happening within our bodies, and within the world that we are eternally connected to. We must listen to that little voice inside when it is trying to help us avoid disaster. I didn't trust that voice before, but now I do. I listen to it, for it is me, loving me.

I feel I'm at the beginning of a new life, just learning how to crawl. I will eventually learn to walk and talk. One day, I will sing and dance. I'll make many mistakes along the way, for I have much to learn about this crazy life. It is frightening at times, and I get weak, but I'm hopeful about what lay ahead. I believe it will get better, for all of us. I know it is going to be beautiful, because I now know that I am beautiful too. I'm very glad I have lived to tell.

Acknowledgements

It took a lifetime of people to help me become the person I am today. I owe a huge thanks to my adoptive parents and my adoptive family who helped to raise me. You are my family, the only family I've ever known and all the family I'll ever need. I don't need to run through a list of names; each one of you knows what you mean to me. And thank you, my birth mother. Though I never knew you, you chose to give me life even though you knew you couldn't take care of that life. You thought of me, and I will always love you for that.

Jeffrey. My Superman. Our relationship is unique. We don't fit any mold. But we love each other, this is for sure. Thank you for never giving up on me!

Thank you, Michael. You not only helped me save myself; you have shown love for me. You've touched my life in ways I could have never expected. You are a good friend.

Heli, Luci, what can I say? You are my ascended master. You are my teacher. You are my sistah. I love you, Girl.

And mbf&b, John Steers. Where do I begin? You've taught me so much through all of this. You are the voice of a community of love that has surrounded and protected me, through more years and times than I probably know. I don't really understand how, and I probably don't need to, but I cherish the love. You've helped me to become a man. Thank you, my brother.

Thank you, Jill Kelly. Having you as my editor, helping me turn my cluster of a manuscript into this book is something I know was meant to be. Our work together has been a very comfortable, enjoyable journey. You've taught me so much about this business of writing. I hope you know how much you mean to me.

And thanks to everyone who betrayed and hurt me. You have been a mirror in my life. You've helped me to understand myself, to better myself, and this world around me. Because of you, I can now see.

Finally, this book is dedicated to everyone who has suffered through the terrible nightmare, a nightmare that has gone on for way too long. I hope the light I shine upon this darkness will help all of us to tell our story and finally set us free.

About the Author

David lives in the Seattle area with his life partner, Jeffrey. He is the Director of Technology for a Seattle media company. When not exploring the planet with Jeff, he can be found obsessing over recipes in the kitchen, digging in the garden, acrylic painting, or reading with his two cats curled up beside him. Visit him online at www.livetotellthebook.com

www.ingramcontent.com/pod-product-compliance
Lightning Source LLC
Chambersburg PA
CBHW020423290526
45785CB00002B/698